Better Homes and Gardens

D0460725

more
incredibly
awesome
crafts
for kids

Better Homes and Gardens® Books, Des Moines, Iowa

Better Homes and Gardens® Books
An imprint of Meredith® Books

More Incredibly Awesome Crafts for Kids
Editor: Carol Field Dahlstrom
Technical Editor: Susan Banker
Graphic Designer: Marisa Terry
Technical Illustrator: Chris Neubauer Graphics
Photographers: Hopkins Associates and Scott Little
Copy Chief: Angela K. Renkoski
Copy Editor: Colleen Johnson
Proofreader: Marcia R. Gilmer
Editorial and Design Assistants: Judy Bailey, Jennifer Norris
Electronic Production Coordinator: Paula Forest
Production Director: Douglas Johnston
Production Manager: Pam Kvitne
Prepress Coordinator: Marjorie J. Schenkelberg

Meredith® Books
Editor in Chief: James D. Blume
Design Director: Matt Strelecki
Managing Editor: Gregory H. Kayko

Vice President, General Manager: Jamie L. Martin

Better Homes and Gardens® Magazine
Editor in Chief: Jean LemMon

Meredith Publishing Group
President, Publishing Group: Christopher M. Little
Vice President and Publishing Director: John P. Loughlin

Meredith Corporation
Chairman of the Board: Jack D. Rehm
President and Chief Executive Officer: William T. Kerr

Chairman of the Executive Committee: E. T. Meredith III

Cover photography: Scott Little, Andy Lyons

All of us at Better Homes and Gardens® Books are dedicated to providing you with the information and ideas you need to create beautiful and useful projects. We guarantee your satisfaction with this book for as long as you own it. We welcome your questions, comments, and suggestions. Please write to us at: Better Homes and Gardens Books, Crafts RW–240, 1716 Locust Street, Des Moines, IA 50309–3023.

get ready! get set!

Go get the scissors, grab tape and the glue,
Find the paint and the markers, get some newspapers, too!

Can you feel the excitement? It's time to create.
With your great ideas, there's no time to wait!

We've got pinwheels and garlands and beads by the yard,
Make a bracelet, a lampshade, a mask, a notecard.

Try your hand at a puppet, a doll, or some shoes,
Paint an egg or a bookworm—you really can't lose!

It's all here to please you, there's lots to be done.
Get ready, get set—and have lots of fun!

hello!

here's what's

❋ Have Fun With Paper

❋ Wear It and Look Great!

paper

wear it

Nature Cap, page 54.
Bedazzling Beads, page 58.

in the book

Fancy Flowerpot, page 130.

✳ Puppets & Dolls to Craft and Love

✳ One, Two, Three Paint!

✳ Gifts to Make All by Yourself

dolls

paint

gifts

5

how to use your book and make cool crafts!

* **Show your mom or dad** what project you'd like to make and make sure the kitchen table will be all yours for a while!

* **Put a smile** on Mom's face by covering your work surface with wax paper, newspapers, a paper bag—anything you can throw away at the end of your crafting.

* **It's also nice** to have paper towels, a damp sponge, and a waste paper basket handy in case of spills and to keep your work area clean.

* **Read through the list** of what you'll need to make your project and gather the supplies. If you need something from the store, be sure to say "please" and "thank you" to Mom or Dad!

* **Before you start,** read through all the project steps and look at the photographs and any diagrams or patterns. (Read the tips, too—they can really help!) If you don't understand a step, just ask a grown-up for help.

* **Our Helping Hand** looks like this: 🖐. That's when you'll need to ask a grown-up for help.

* **All of the patterns are full size** to make sure all your projects turn out just right. With your imagination, these patterns could be used for hundreds of other crafts!

* **Start with Step "1"** and keep going until you are done.

* Most of all ...**HAVE FUN** creating your very own incredibly awesome crafts!!

have fun with paper

It comes in bright colors
and soft shades, too.
It's fun just to cut,
color, and glue.

We've got snowflakes
and pinwheels and boxes galore.
There are garlands and frames
and lampshades and more.

Whatever you make,
whatever you do—
It will always be special
'cause it's made by you!

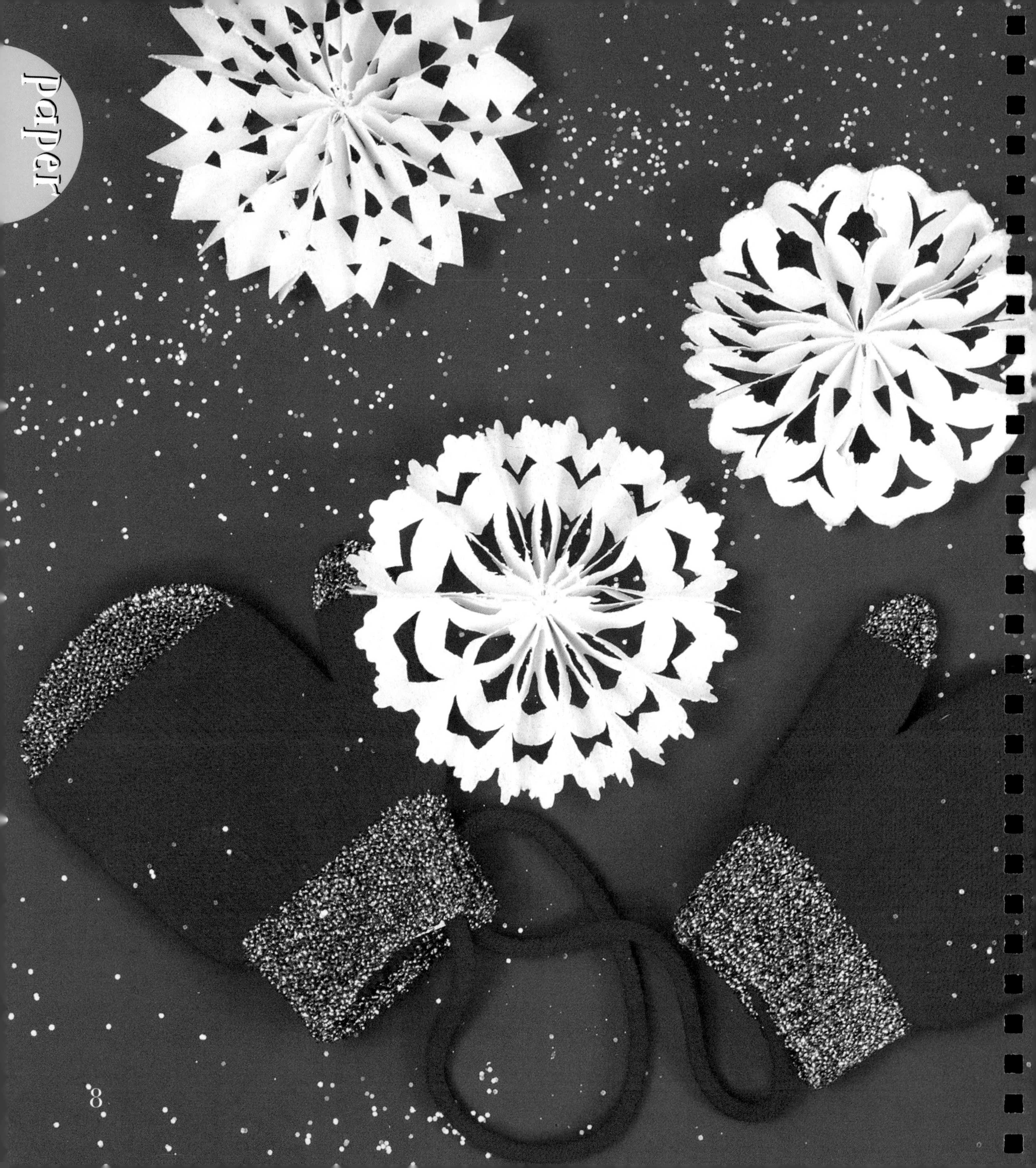

Did you know?

* You can make your own snow cone by pouring orange juice over clean snow in a cup.
* A snowflake is the only creation in all of nature that is formed instantly.

sparkly snowflakes

Create your own glittering, white, geometric snowflakes any time of the year! These three-dimensional, sparkly paper snowflakes are just like the icy cold variety—no two will ever be the same. Turn the page to learn how to make them.

sparkly snowflakes

you'll need...

Lightweight typing paper
Scissors
Pencil
Lightweight string
Glue stick
White glitter

1 Fold a piece of typing paper in half, with the LONG EDGES together.

2 Unfold the paper and cut along the fold line.

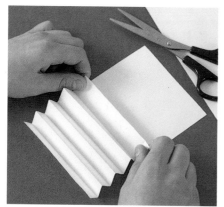

3 Starting at the short end, fold the paper like a fan every ¾ inch, keeping the edges even.

4 Trace a pattern from *page 11* on one end of the paper or draw your own snowflake design.

5 Cut out the center notch as shown on the patterns. The notch lets the snowflake open and glue easily. Tie a piece of string around the notch.

tip: Be sure to draw the pattern so both sides have some of the design on a fold or your snowflake will fall apart.

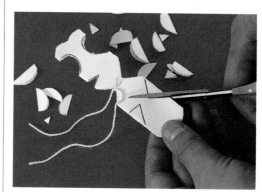

6 Continue cutting out the black sections as shown on the pattern.

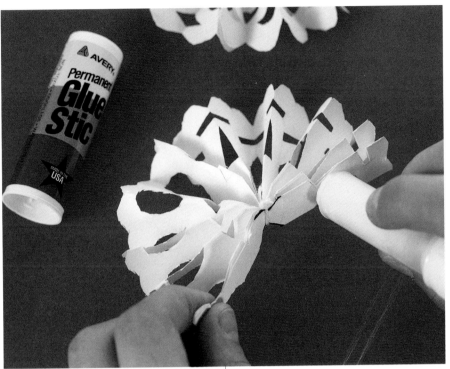

tip:
The pattern does not have to be the same on both sides of the notch to work but it will fit best if it is.

Trace these nifty snowflake patterns!

7 Fold the paper ends together and glue. Trim the string or use it to hang the snowflake.

8 Glue glitter to the snowflake edges or on the front of the snowflake.

tip:
Try using various craft scissors to create zigzags and scallops around the outer edge.

Fold

Center Notch

Fold

Fold

Center Notch

Fold

Fold

Center Notch

Fold

Remember to fold along the dotted lines!

pinwheel pizzazz

Now you can make your own special pinwheel—in the colors you choose— and play for hours outside in the wind (or make it move with your own wind). Try to make one ... it's a breeze!

you'll need...

Pencil
Ruler
Scrap piece of wrapping
    paper
Scissors
A penny
12-inch piece of ¼-inch-square
    balsa wood
Marking pens
Straight pin with large
    plastic head
Large pony bead
Eraser from end of pencil
Curling ribbons to match
    wrapping paper

pinwheel pizzazz

1 With a pencil and ruler, mark an 8-inch square on the back side of the wrapping paper. Cut out the square.

2 Draw pencil lines from corner to corner on the back of the paper (like a big "X").

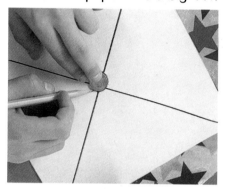

3 Place the penny in the center of the "X" on the back of the wrapping paper and draw around it.

4 Fold all four corners to the center, creasing the folds as you go.

5 Using your scissors, cut between the folded triangles as shown in the photo above—being careful to cut up to, but NOT THROUGH the center circle you drew. (You'll have four cuts when you are done cutting.)

6 Decorate the wood piece for the handle however you wish using marking pens. (You can even glue on gems!)

7 Cut eight pieces of curling ribbon, each about 8 inches long. Use a scissor to curl ends (ask an adult for a helping hand).

Did you Know?

✷ Pinwheels are really modeled after windmills and need wind (or your blowing air) to move.

✷ Pinwheels used to be called "whirligigs."

Put your pinwheel together like this!

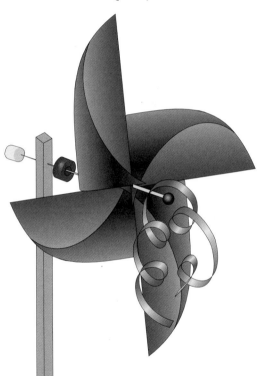

8 Bend (DO NOT FOLD) every other point to the center of the square as shown in the photograph *above*.

9 Push the pin through the center of the curling ribbons, then through all four points of the pinwheel, one at a time. Then push the pin through the center of the square.

tip: If the curling ribbon keeps the pinwheel from moving freely, cut the ends a little shorter.

10 Place a pony bead onto the pin, behind the pinwheel. Next, push the pin through one end of the wood handle, about ½ inch from the end. Carefully push the eraser onto the end of the pin.

11 If you'd like, decorate the pinwheel blades using stickers and more ribbon.

tip: You could poke your pin into a small cork instead of a pencil eraser.

15

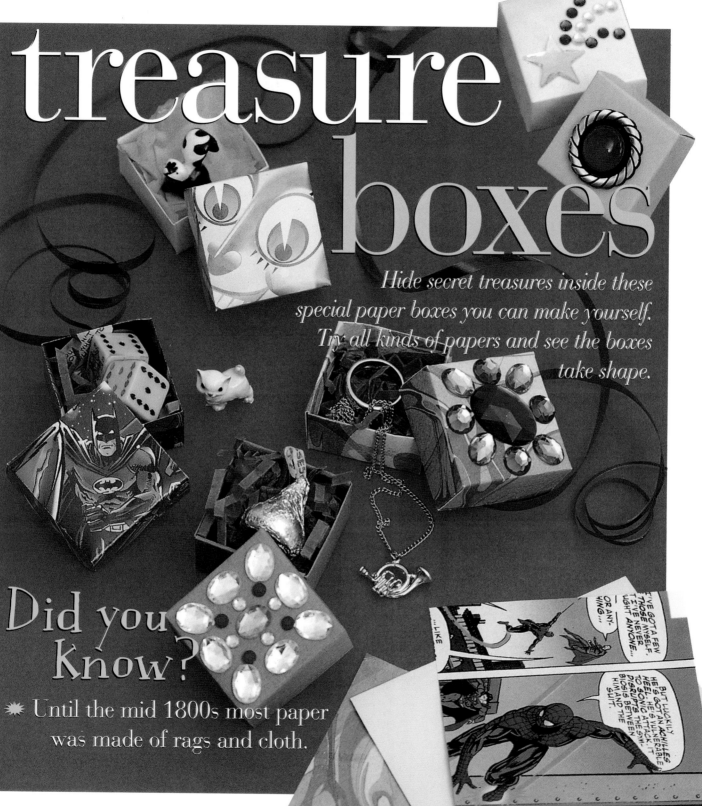

treasure boxes

Hide secret treasures inside these special paper boxes you can make yourself. Try all kinds of papers and see the boxes take shape.

Did you Know?

✹ Until the mid 1800s most paper was made of rags and cloth.

16

you'll need...

Medium-weight craft paper,
comic books, or
magazines
Ruler
Pencil
Scissors
Crafts glue
Decorations for box top such
as jewels and stickers

1 Measure and cut out one 4½-inch square for the box top and one 4¼-inch square for the box bottom.

2 Draw an "X" across the back of both squares, corner to corner.

3 Using one paper square, fold one corner to the center of the "X."

tip: Be sure to crease the folds with your fingernail so you get easy-to-see folds.

4 Fold the same section again to the center line. Unfold the paper and repeat with each of the other three corners.

5 Repeat Steps 3 and 4 for the second paper square.

6 Refer to the diagram on *page 18*, then on both paper squares make four cuts into the square along the fold lines (we've drawn them in so you could see them better). Be sure not to cut into the blue-colored center square as shown on the diagram!

7 Fold in the sides that are shaped like big triangles and bend the corners to form the sides of the box.

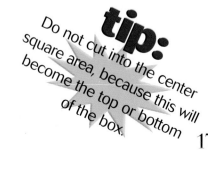

8 Fold the other two sections over the sides and tuck them in on the inside of the box. Use a dab of glue to hold.

9 Decorate the top of the box if you like, using glue to attach any jewels. Put the lid on the bottom of the box.

tip: Do not cut into the center square area, because this will become the top or bottom of the box.

17

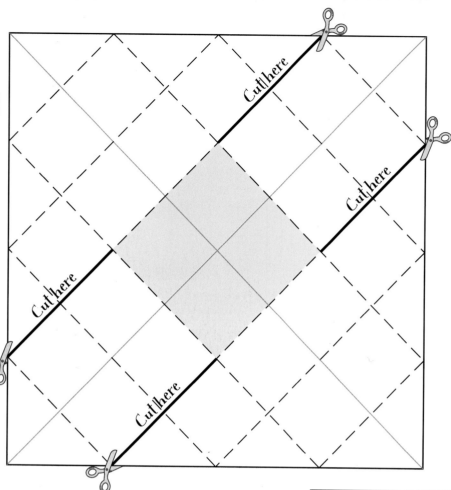

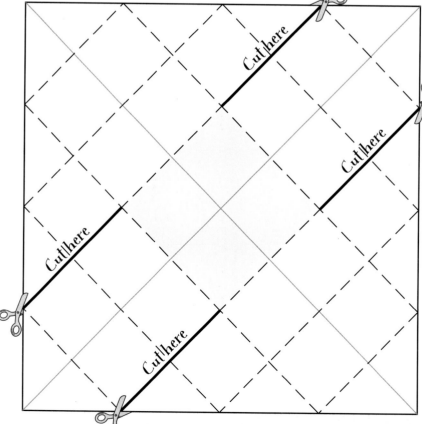

Cut here
Cut here
Cut here
Cut here

Use this diagram to make the lid of your treasure box. The dotted lines are the fold lines.

Use this diagram to make the bottom of your treasure box. The dotted lines are the fold lines.

Cut here
Cut here
Cut here
Cut here

18

magic garlands

*With long, narrow paper and just
a snip of your scissors, you can create
magic garlands that seem to go on forever!
Turn the page to learn how.*

Did you Know?

✱ The Chinese were the first to use cut
paper for making lamps, lanterns,
and window coverings.

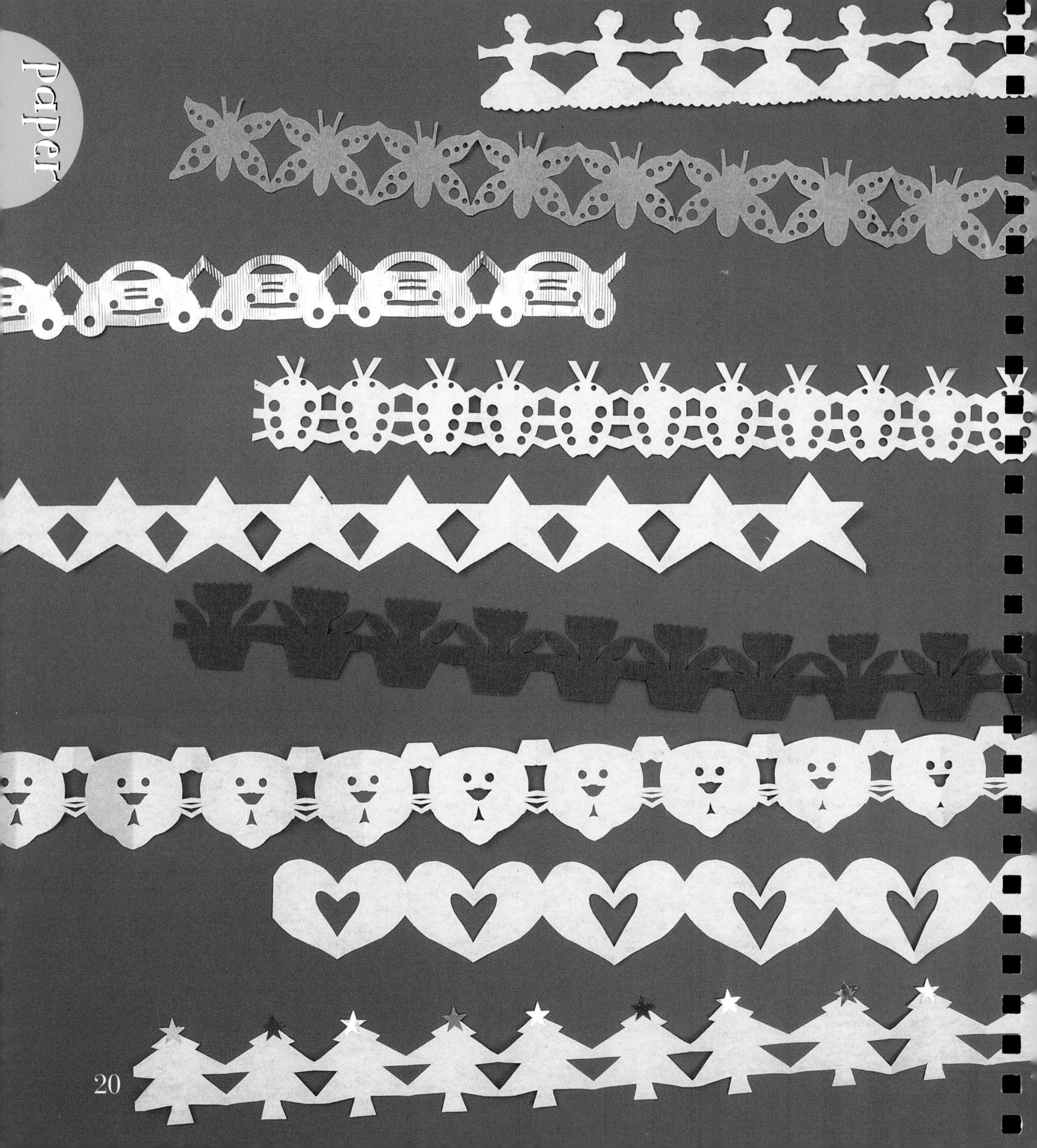

magic garlands

Pencil
White typing paper
Paper to make the garlands:
   Streamer, adding machine,
   or typing paper
Scissors
Pinking shears or scalloped
   scissors, if desired
Round paper punches

1 Trace the pattern you like from *pages 22–23* on typing paper, coloring in the black areas. Cut out the traced pattern around the four edges.

2 Lay your traced pattern under the garland paper, matching the edge to the end of the strip. Trace your pattern again on the end of your strip.

3 Fold the paper like a fan where the design ends, keeping the edges even as you fold. Fold as many times as you wish (not too many though, or it is too hard to cut!).

4 Trim the top (unfolded edge) of the paper using pinking shears IF making the flower. Trim the bottom using a scallop scissors IF making the dancer.

tip:
If not using streamer or adding machine paper, you can cut strips of typing or tissue paper about 2¼x11 inches.

5 Using the pencil lines as a guide, cut away the areas between the lines (shown as the dark areas on the pattern).

tip:
The trick to successful garlands is to be sure both sides have folds that don't get cut.

6 If the pattern has small round dots in the design, punch these out last using paper punches.

Did you Know?

✳ In Mexico cut paper designs are thought to bring good luck.

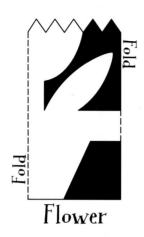

Flower

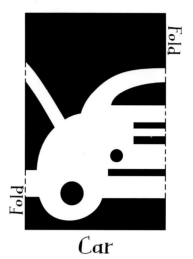

Car

Cat

Have fun
tracing these
patterns to make
paper garlands!

Ladybug

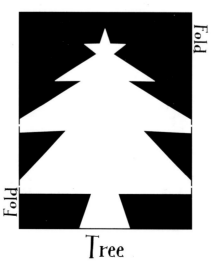

Tree

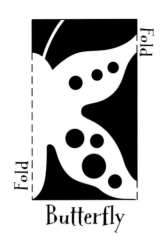

Fold

Fold

Butterfly

Fold

Fold

Heart

Fold

Fold

Dancer

Remember, the
dotted lines are the
fold lines!

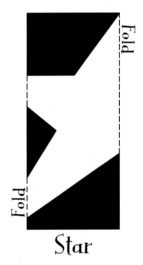

Fold

Fold

Star

Fold

Fold

Snowman

23

Bertram the bird ~ piñata

It's always such fun to have a party with a new friend—meet Bertram the Piñata (you don't have to break him to get the candy out; you can just take the tape off the bottom). Learn how to make Bertram on pages 26–27.

24

you'll need...

Large oval-shaped balloon
About 1 cup of water
About 1 cup of flour
Container to hold the
    water and flour mixture
Newspaper
Wide masking tape
Black marker
Acrylic or tempera paint:
    white and black
Paintbrush
3 packages of yellow tissue
    paper (in all one color or
    multicolored yellows)
Pencil with new eraser
White crafts glue
Disposable plate
Typing paper
Three 8½x11-inch
    pieces of orange
    construction paper
Yellow feathers
Wrapped candy

25

bird piñata

Papier-mâché

You will be making your bird piñata out of papier-mâché. Papier-mâché is a French word that means "chewed or pulped paper." The mix of paper and a glue is often used to build sculptures like Bertram. We are using strips of newspaper and a flour and water mixture (for our glue) to make our papier-mâché. When the papier-mâché dries, it will be very hard.

1 Measure about 1 cup of water and pour it into your container. Measure and add about 1 cup of flour to the water (always add the flour to the water). Mix the water and flour until it is thick like gravy, adding more flour if needed.

2 Tear or cut the newspaper into strips that are about 1½ inches wide.

3 Blow up the balloon and tie it. With a black marker, draw a circle on the bottom, about 3 inches in diameter, to help you remember to leave this hole uncovered.

4 Dip each strip of newspaper into the flour mixture and put it directly onto the balloon. Cover the entire balloon with strips of paper going in all directions, EXCEPT leave the hole you marked uncovered. Let this layer dry.

5 After the first layer is dry, make the eyes by wadding up two little pieces of newspaper about the size of a bouncy ball. Tape these to the dry papier-mâché with masking tape where you want the eyes to be. Now start the second layer of papier-mâché by dipping the newspaper into the flour mixture and placing it over the eyes and all over the balloon again, remembering not to cover the hole. Allow this layer to dry.

6 If you want your piñata to be extra-strong, apply a third coat. Always be sure to leave the hole uncovered. The balloon may begin to shrink a little, but that is all right.

Did you know?

✳ Early Spanish piñatas were clay jugs called "ollas." that usually held water or food.

✳ Piñatas originated in Italy.

7 After the last layer is dry, pop the balloon—this is fun! Reach in the hole and pull out the remains of the balloon. Fill the papier-mâché sphere with wrapped candies and tape over the hole securely with masking tape.

8 Using the white paint, paint the eyes. Put a black dot in the middle of the eye with a white dot highlight. Using black paint, paint a large circle in the center of the piñata. This is where the beak will go after the tissue paper is on the piñata.

9 Cut the tissue paper into squares that are about 2x2 inches square. It doesn't matter if these are cut perfectly. The size can vary a little. You will need a lot of these squares (at least 100), so cut several of them at once. With good scissors, you can layer at least five or six pieces of tissue paper at a time and cut through all of the layers.

10 Mark a 3-inch circle where you painted the black paint. You will not cover this part, because the beak will go here when you are done. Also, leave an area without tissue paper at the bottom of the bird where the tape is (about a 3-inch circle), so you can glue the feet to the bottom of the bird.

11 You are now ready to cover your piñata with tissue squares. To make your fluffy tissue feathers, put some glue on a disposable plate. Using the eraser end of the pencil, wrap a tissue square around the pencil and dip it into the glue. Put the pencil with the tissue and glue onto the piñata. Do this again and again (and again!), placing the little pieces close together. It will take a lot of time to cover the whole balloon. Remember to leave the spots for the beak and feet.

12 Trace the beak and feet patterns on *pages 28–29* onto typing paper and cut out. Lay these patterns onto the orange paper and cut out two feet and two beak pieces.

13 Fold the beak pieces as marked on the pattern. Glue the beak pieces on the piñata on the black paint that you left without tissue paper. Glue the feet to the bottom of the bird where you left a spot. Glue some feathers on top of his head in between some of the tissue.

Trace this pattern to make Bertram's beak.

Piñata Beak
Cut 2

Fold

Fold

Fold

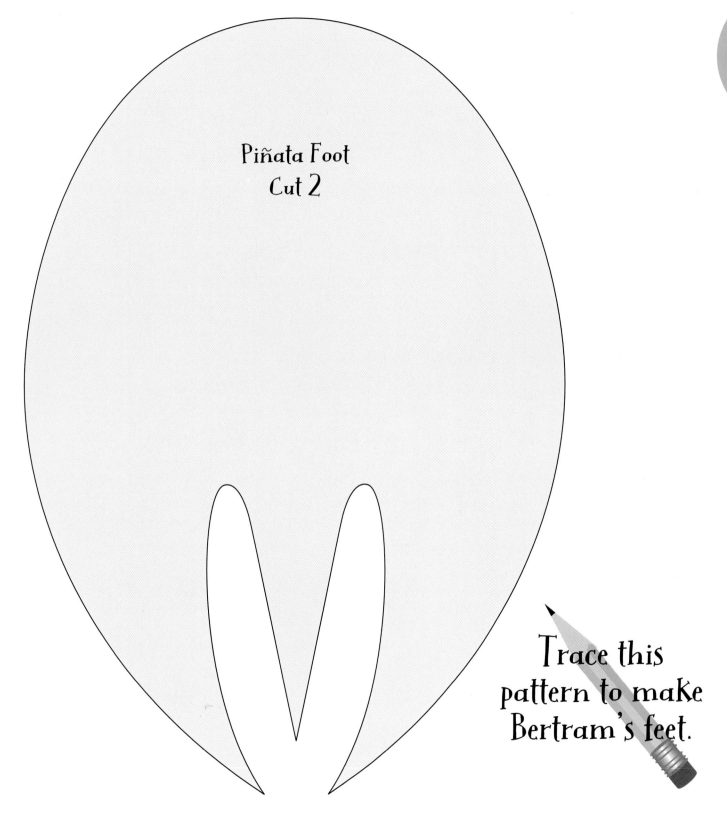

Piñata Foot
Cut 2

Trace this
pattern to make
Bertram's feet.

29

Want to see more of your friends? Now you can see them every day as they smile at you on frames, lampshades, and note cards. Turn the page and learn how to make all three projects.

picture
pals

Did you Know?

❋ The first copies were made by putting ink on carved wooden blocks and pressing them on paper.

❋ The first electrophotographic copier (that's a mouthful!) was patented in 1942.

how to get copies of your photos and make a photo collage...

1 Cut out pictures of your friends from school pictures or snapshots. (If you don't want to cut up your photos, copy the entire snapshot and trim the copy. Then copy the trimmed copy.)

2 Arrange and overlap pictures, turning some upside down and sideways, onto a piece of typing paper. (It's OK if some of the paper shows through.)

3 Use a glue stick to spot-glue the pictures in place.

4 Ask your parents to take you to a photocopy store and make several black and white copies of your photo collage. (You may have to lighten the contrast of the machine. It's easy to do—just ask for help.)

31

picture pals projects

picture frame

you'll need...

White crafts glue
8x10-inch oval photo mat
   with cardboard backing
Copied black and white
   photo collage
Mod Podge decoupage sealer
Paintbrush
Tape
Typing paper
Pencil
9x4-inch piece of medium-
   weight cardboard for stand
Colorful rubber bands

1 Apply the glue evenly to the front of the photo mat. Lay the photo collage, right side up, over the mat and smooth it in place with your fingers.

tip: Put a piece of waxed paper under the frame when you are applying the Mod Podge to keep your table clean.

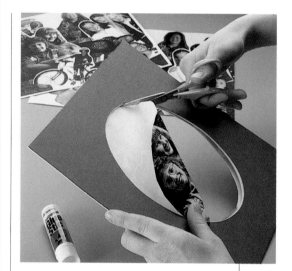

2 Trim away any excess paper from around the outside edge and inside the oval opening. Let the glue dry.

3 Paint on several coats of Mod Podge over the collage. Let it dry between coats.

4 Place the oval mat over the picture to be framed. Tape the picture in place at the top edge on the back.

5 Place the backing cardboard behind the picture. Use rubber bands to hold the layers in place.

6 Trace the photo stand pattern on *page 34* onto typing paper; cut it out. Draw around the pattern on the medium-weight piece of cardboard and cut it out.

7 Fold the stand as shown on the pattern on *page 34*.

tip: Try making your own wrapping paper by using photo copies of family, friends—even pets!

8 Center the stand on the back of the frame. Matching the stand bottom to the bottom edge of the frame, glue down the bottom and the top tabs.

lampshade

you'll need...

Copied black and white
   photo collage
Small lampshade with
   smooth surface
Magic tape (Scotch or 3M)
White crafts glue
Typing paper
Mod Podge decoupage sealer
Paintbrush
Black single-edge bias tape

1 Cut apart the photo collage sections. Arrange them on the lampshade how you want them and tape in place for now.

2 When the shade is covered, remove one piece at a time. To glue, place each piece face down on a piece of clean typing paper and apply glue evenly over each piece.

3 Press each glued piece onto the shade and smooth it with your fingers to be sure that all edges are glued down. Repeat with the other cut-out pieces, using a clean piece of paper for each gluing.

4 Allow the shade to dry completely and use a paintbrush to cover it with several coats of Mod Podge, letting it dry between coats.

5 Glue a strip of black bias tape around the top edge of the lampshade, overlapping the ends of the tape at the back of the shade.

note card

you'll need...

9x6-inch piece of paper
   folded to a 4½x6-inch card
Copied black and white
   photo collage
Glue stick
Colored pencils

1 Cut a shape from the photo collage that is at least ½ inch smaller than the size of the card front. Use a glue stick to glue the collage to the note card.

2 Use colored pencils to color in whatever areas you would like on your photo collage. Have fun and try using unusual colors—like blue or green for hair!

33

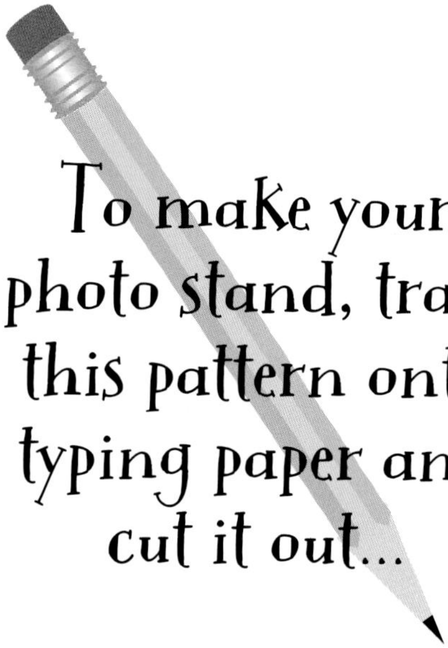

To make your photo stand, trace this pattern onto typing paper and cut it out...

then draw around the pattern on the medium-weight piece of cardboard and cut out.

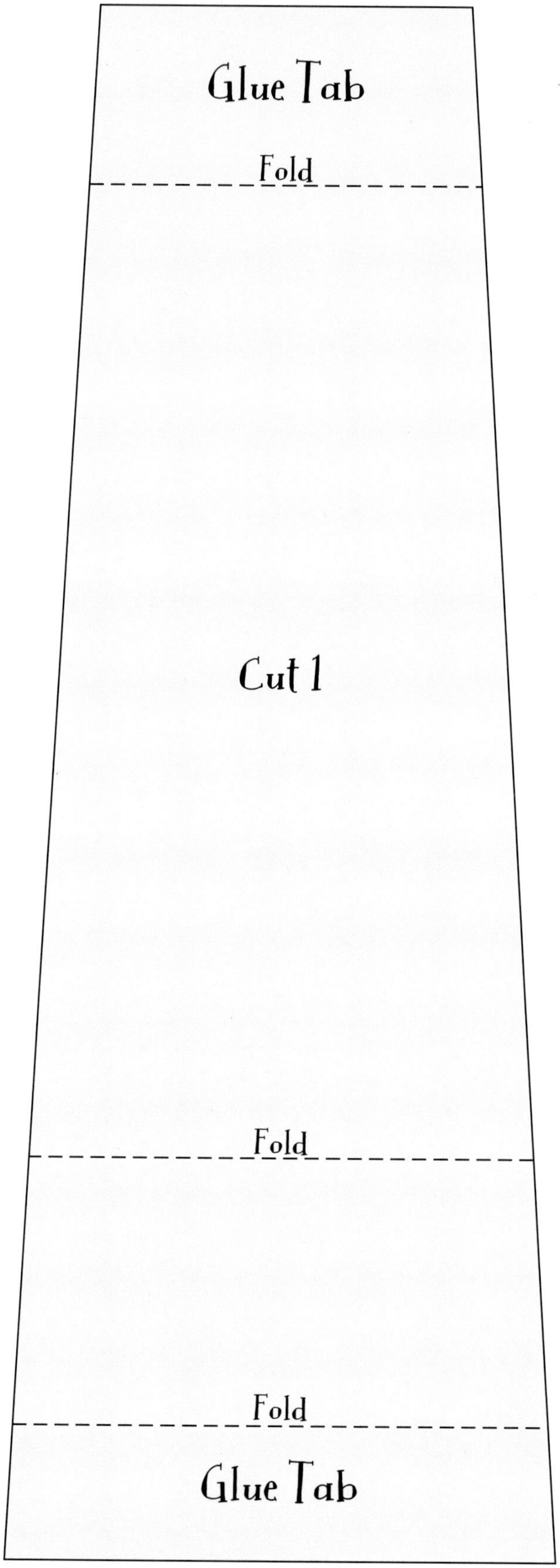

Glue Tab

Fold

Cut 1

Fold

Fold

Glue Tab

wear it
and look great!

There are beads to be strung
and hats to be worn.
There are shoes to be laced
and vests to adorn.

You've done it! You've made it!
It's all just so right.
The colors are perfect,
the design—out of sight!

So wear it and love it
and announce right out loud,
"I made it myself
and I'm very proud!"

button, button, who's got the button?

We've got the button and so do you! Look in Grandma's button box or the bags of buttons at the fabric store, and you'll be a button lover forever. We've got all kinds of great wearable button projects for you to make—turn the page and learn how.

This button is made out of vegetable ivory—a substance from a tropical palm tree. These buttons were first made about 1860 and are usually extra-smooth.

This is an early plastic button made in the 1940s. Often they were made in bright colors. Can you find some others?

This is a novelty button that looks like a bow. It was made about 1950. It has two holes in the back to sew it on.

This is a metal button, probably from a little boy's pair of overalls that were worn about 1910. Look for the other metal buttons on this page.

These buttons were made from glass and were probably sewn on a baby dress in about 1900. Glass buttons are old. Some date to the 1700s.

This button has rhinestones on it and was probably worn on a fancy party dress in about 1940.

This button is a pearl button—it was made from an oyster shell. What other buttons do you see that were made from shells?

wear it

HOME SPUN

37

button
bracelets

Wear your button bracelets on both wrists and steal the show! They are fun and simple to make. For help with how to sew on a button, turn the page.

you'll need...

1-inch-wide elastic
Sewing thread
Needle
Buttons in the colors and
shapes you like

1 Cut a piece of elastic that is 2 inches longer than your wrist. Pick out buttons you wish to use on your bracelet. Try using similar colors, buttons with the same theme (like flowers or bugs), or striped buttons.

2 Sew the first button on about 1 inch from the end of the elastic. (For help with how to sew on a button, look on *pages 40–41*.) Continue sewing buttons all over the elastic until it is covered EXCEPT for 1 inch at each end.

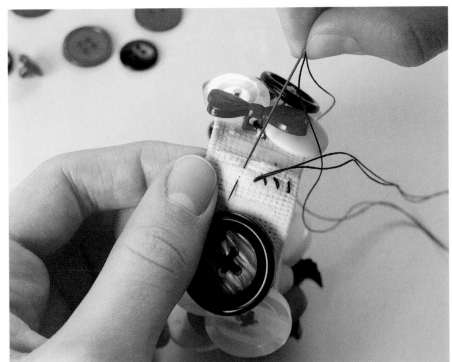

3 Overlap the ends of the elastic, then use little stitches to sew your bracelet together. Sew over it again and again to hold.

tip:
If using both shank and 2- or 4-hole buttons, sew on the holed buttons first, filling in blank areas using the shank buttons.

4 Cover the stitches by sewing on more buttons.

Did you Know?

✹ The first buttons can be traced back to ancient Egypt.

how to sew on a 2- or 4-hole button

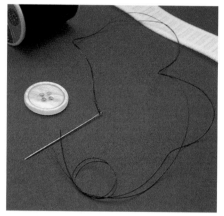

1 Thread an 18-inch piece of thread through the needle. Bring the ends of the thread together and tie a knot at the end.

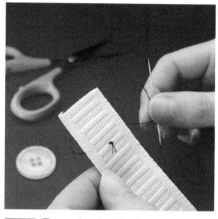

2 From the back side of the fabric (or elastic, as in our example), push the needle through to the front. Pull until the knot is firm against the back side.

3 Put the sewing needle through one hole (it doesn't matter which one) in the back of the 2- or 4-hole button.

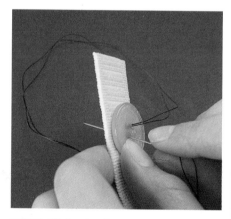

4 Slide the button close to the fabric and insert the needle into the opposite hole on the button. Push the needle through the fabric. Repeat three times.

5 For 4-hole buttons, bring the needle up again through a third hole. Then push the needle back through the last hole and the fabric. Repeat three times.

6 To finish, run the needle through the stitches on the back side again and again to keep the button and threads in place. Clip the thread ends.

wear it

These are shank buttons!

This is the shank!

how to sew on a shank button

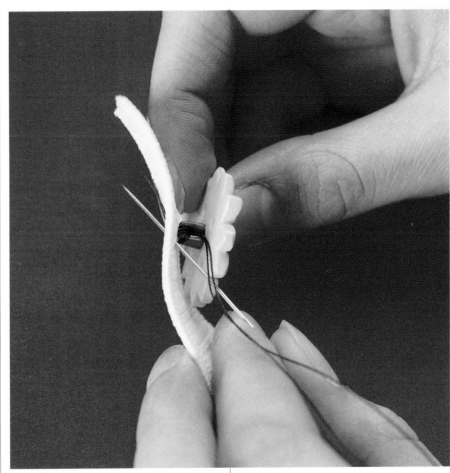

1 Thread the needle and tie the ends together in a knot. Push the needle from the back to the front of the fabric (or elastic), as shown on *page 40*. Slip the threaded needle through the shank and through the front of the fabric (or elastic) to the back.

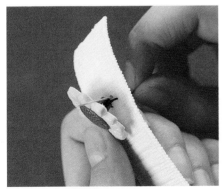

2 Push the needle through the fabric to the front again, close to the first stitch.

3 Push the needle through the button shank a second time and bring the needle to the back. Repeat at least three times. Finish as for the 2- or 4-hole button.

tip: To thread a needle quickly, fold the thread in half and push the looped end through the needle eye.

41

What a beautiful button garden you can grow—and your friends won't believe you made it yourself! Learn how on the next page.

flower garden vest

you'll need...

Denim vest with yokes
Chalk
Assorted colorful and/or
   flower-shaped buttons
Various colors of thread
Green paint pen

1 Wash the vest and let it dry. If putting the vest in the clothes dryer, DO NOT use a fabric softener sheet. (If you put fabric softener in with your vest, the paint may not stick.)

2 Using chalk, mark "Xs" on the vest yolks to show where you want your button flowers to go. Look at the photo on *page 42* for ideas.

Look at the photo on *page 42* for ideas.

3 Use your favorite colors of thread to sew on buttons where you marked the "Xs."

4 To make the stems for your button flowers, use a green paint pen to draw lines from your button flowers to the seam of your vest yoke (or wherever you want your flowers to be "planted"). To make the leaves, draw teardrop shapes next to the stems. Let the paint dry completely.

Be sure to read the label on your paint pen. Some paints need to be "set" using an iron. Ask a grown-up for a helping hand if you have this kind of paint.

tip: You could also add button flowers to pockets, a cap, a purse flap—even sock cuffs!

Did you know?

✹ In the olden days, a vest was called a "waistcoat."

glamour rings

Every finger deserves such a button beauty! So easy to make, you'll want to make some for your friends!

Utility scissors
Colored pipe cleaners
Decorative shank buttons

1 For each ring, cut a piece of pipe cleaner 4 inches long. Thread a button onto the pipe cleaner and push the button to the center.

2 Wrap the pipe cleaner around your finger to shape the ring. Twist the ends of the pipe cleaner once to make it the right size.

3 Take the ring off your finger and trim the ends of the pipe cleaner to measure about ¼ inch long. Twist the trimmed pipe cleaner ends around the rest of the pipe cleaner ring to hold the ends in place.

tip: Be sure to tuck the wire of the pipe cleaner around to the back so it doesn't poke you.

Did you Know?

✳ In 1860, buttons replaced lace as the favorite trimming on ladies' dresses.

✳ Long ago, wearing pearl buttons was a sign of daintiness.

shoes
and laces

You'll be standing proud as everyone looks down—only to admire your awesome shoes and laces! For lots of ideas that will give you jazzy, snazzy feet, turn the page.

46

Did you Know?

✳ In the early 1800s, women wore ballerina-like slippers that laced on to make their feet seem as small as possible.

wear it

47

lively laces

Your shoes will be so happy all laced up with shoelaces designed by you!
They're easy to make—learn how on the next page.

you'll need...

Waxed paper or a
   grocery bag
White flat shoelaces (sold for
   athletic shoes)
Permanent markers in
   assorted colors

1 Cover your work table
with waxed paper or a
grocery bag before you start to
color. Then, just in case you
slip, you won't get marker on
your table.

2 If your shoelace is hard to
color on because it
moves around too much, tape
the lace ends to your work
surface before you begin.

tip:
Try not to color on the plastic
ends of your laces because it
might rub off and get messy.

3 Using permanent
markers, decorate one
side of each shoelace with a
bright pattern or stripes. Let the
marker dry. Repeat the design
on the other side of the lace.

tip:
Don't hold the marker on
the lace too long or it will soak
through to the other side.

Did you Know?

✴ The first shoes were actually sandals that were held
in place by laces around the ankles.

cartoon sneakers

wear it

All eyes will be on your feet when you wear your personalized and silly cartoon shoes. Pick your favorite cartoon character and have fun turning those old sneakers into something special.

you'll need...

Cartoon section of the
   Sunday newspaper
Scissors
Canvas tennis shoes
Pencil
Paintbrush
Mod Podge decoupage
   sealer
Spoon
Red paint pen for fabric

1 Cut out your favorite characters from the cartoon section of the Sunday newspaper. Decide what parts of your shoes you want to cover and draw lines around those areas. Using the paintbrush, brush a smooth coat of Mod Podge over the parts you outlined to seal the shoe. Let the Mod Podge dry. (We covered the toe and heel, then added cutouts on each side.)

2 Arrange the cartoons on the shoe, putting Mod Podge under and over each piece. You can smooth the paper with the back of a spoon as you go. You also can put your hand inside the shoe to hold it still while you're smoothing out the paper.

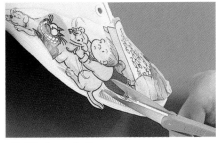

3 Carefully cut away any paper that is outside the area you want to cover. Also, cut away any paper that goes over the edge of the rubber sole. Rub the paper edges back down using the spoon.

4 After the Mod Podge is dry, brush on three more coats, letting the shoes dry between each coat.

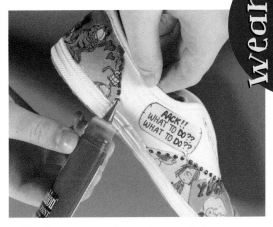

5 Decorate the edges of the cartoons with dots of red paint, like we did, or add squiggles and dots wherever you wish.

tip:
To clean your cartoon sneakers, just wipe them off with a damp cloth and a little soap.

Did you Know?

✻ In the 1950s, it was popular to wear thick crepe-soled shoes called "beetle crushers."
✻ The first shoes were sometimes made from a piece of animal hide or heavy paper.

51

hats, shirts, and jewelry

*Hats off to you! You're all dressed up
in things you've made all by yourself—and you look
great! For ideas and instructions for fun-to-make
wearables, turn the page.*

Did you know?

✳ People who make men's hats are called "hatters," and those who make women's hats are called "milliners."

wear it

BUTTERFLIES AND MOTHS

A Study of the Largest and Most Beautiful of the Insects

7806

69¢

53

Did you Know?
✳ Tipping your hat shows respect.

wear it

nature caps

Tracing paper
Pencil
Index cards
Scissors
Scraps of felt in various colors
Hole punch (for star cap)
Cotton baseball cap
Hand towel
Narrow rickrack
Extra-tacky crafts glue
Black fine-tip marker

1 Use a pencil to trace the star, butterfly, or any of the patterns from *pages 56–57* onto tracing paper. Trace each of the pieces separately if the shape has more than one part. Place each traced pattern on an index card and draw around it again. Cut it out. This will make a heavier pattern to trace around on your felt.

tip:
Use permanent marker or paint pen to add eyes or other details to the shapes.

2 Place the pattern shapes on the felt pieces using the colors you like. Draw around them. Use the hole punch to make felt dots for the stars if you wish.

3 Stuff the cap firmly with the towel so the crown holds its shape, making it easier to glue on the rickrack or the felt shapes.

4 To add rickrack, glue it along the seams on the crown and around the bill where it joins the crown.

wear it

5 Glue felt dots to each star. For other layered designs, glue the felt pieces on top of one another as shown on the pattern and *below*.

6 Glue the felt pieces to the cap, using the photograph on *page 54* as a guide to help you decide where you want the shapes to go.

Butterfly

Here is an example of how to cut out and glue layered pattern pieces!

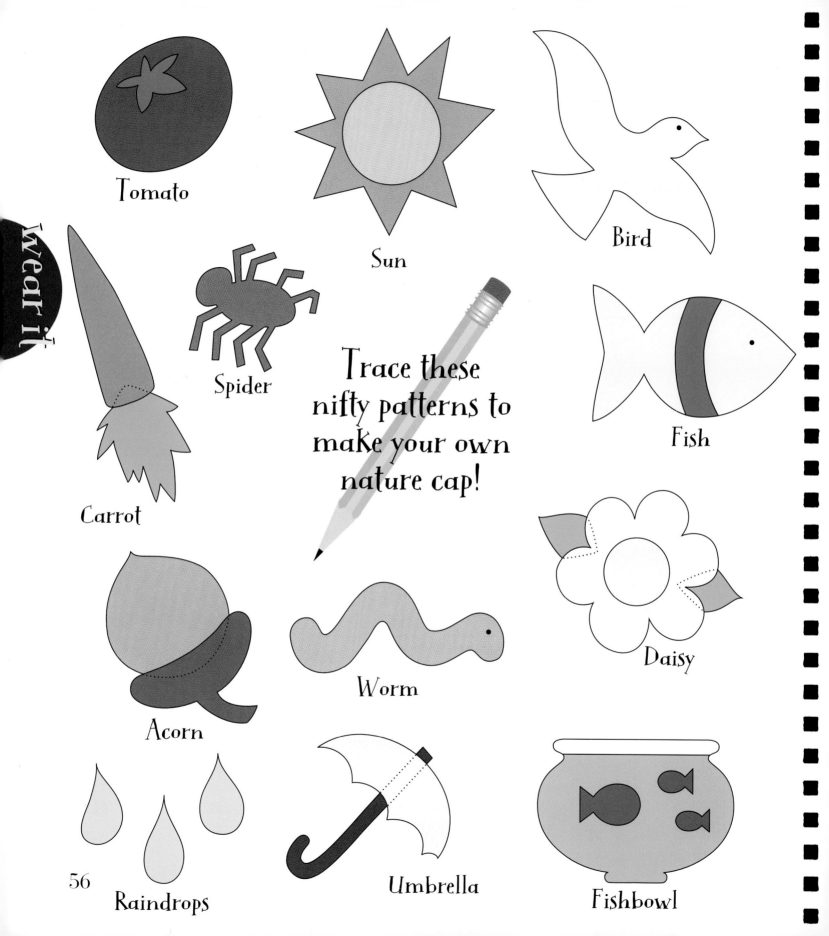

Tomato

Sun

Bird

wear it

Spider

Fish

Carrot

Trace these nifty patterns to make your own nature cap!

Acorn

Worm

Daisy

56

Raindrops

Umbrella

Fishbowl

Tulip

Leaf

Palm Tree

Evergreen

Turtle

Tree

Sunglasses

Heart

Star

Mushroom

Apple

Butterfly

wear it

57

bedazzling beads

wear it

*Easy to make and fun to design,
these beads are made with
ingredients from your kitchen.
To learn how to make the beads,
turn the page.*

Did you Know?

✳ The first dyes were made from
   plants and insects.
✳ Long, long ago (about the year
   1000), "jewelers" were the
   people who added ornamentation
   to shoes for the rich.

bedazzling beads

you'll need...

A recipe of magic clay, below
Plastic drinking straws
Table knife
Toothpicks
Food coloring
Flat pan or cookie sheet

magic clay

you'll need...

2 cups baking soda
1 cup cornstarch
1¼ cups cold water
Aluminum foil

 Have a grown-up give you a helping hand to make the clay. You can keep the clay in a plastic bag in the refrigerator if you want to make the beads later. (But don't let anyone eat it!)

Stir together the baking soda and cornstarch in a saucepan until it is all mixed up. Add the water and stir it again. Cook over medium heat, stirring constantly, until the mixture looks like moist mashed potatoes (about 10 or 15 minutes). Carefully pour it onto the foil and cover it with a damp cloth. Allow the clay to cool. When cool, your clay is ready to make into beads. Keep the clay covered or in a plastic bag until you're ready to use it.

1 To make individual beads, break off a piece of the clay about the size of a large marble. Shape the bead however you wish.

2 Cut the plastic straws into pieces about 4 inches long. Use the straw to make the hole in the middle of the clay. The clay will get stuck in the middle of the straw. When that straw doesn't work any longer, use another piece of straw.

3 Use a toothpick dipped in your choice of food coloring to make lines and dots on the clay.

4 Lay the beads on a cookie sheet to air-dry. They will dry and be very hard in about 6 hours or overnight.

tip: Be sure to cover your work surface before you begin because food coloring sometimes stains.

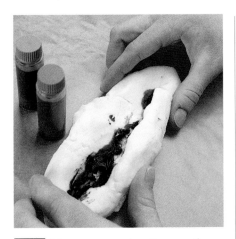

5 You may color the entire batch of clay any color or colors you wish by adding food coloring and kneading it in. Or, you can marbleize the clay in this way: Shape a piece of clay into a hot dog bun shape. Put some food coloring in the middle and scrunch it all together. Shape it into a log shape for slicing, or just break off pieces of the clay to make individual beads.

6 If you choose to slice the beads, slice them using a table knife. Slice the beads about ½ inch thick. Use the pieces of drinking straw to make the holes as you did before. Let these beads dry just as you did the other beads.

7 After the beads are dry, thread them onto yarn, plastic lacing, or any string you wish. We added colorful purchased beads between our clay beads. Tie the ends of the yarn or string into a knot so the beads don't fall off.

tip: If you cover your cookie sheet with foil, it will be easier to clean up!

tip: Because baking soda has a lot of salt in it, your hands will get dry. Have some lotion handy to keep your hands from drying out.

61

Household utensils make great stamping designs
when dipped into your favorite paint colors.
No two shirts will ever be the same!
Instructions are on the next page.

stamp-it
fun shirt

Solid-colored cotton shirt
Waxed paper
Fabric paints in your
    favorite colors
Paper plates
Plastic spoon
Typing paper
Kitchen utensils (we used
    two types of potato
    mashers, a cup, and a
    bottle sponge)

1 Wash and dry your shirt before you begin stamping. (DO NOT use any fabric softener or the paint may peel off.)

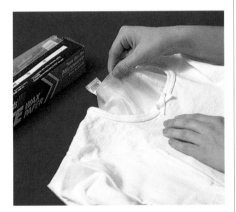

2 Cut pieces of waxed paper to fit inside the shirt body and sleeves. Slide the waxed paper pieces between the two layers of fabric. This will keep the fabric layers separated so the paint doesn't soak through to the back side.

3 Squeeze paint on the paper plates, putting one color on each plate. Smooth the paint out using a plastic spoon. Dab a kitchen utensil in the paint until the bottom is covered. Before you paint your shirt, experiment on a piece of typing paper. Set the painted utensil on the paper and gently pull up. Try each utensil to decide which shapes are your favorites. Then you're ready to start your shirt.

tip: Use only metal or throwaway utensils because paint may ruin wood or plastic utensils.

wear it

4 You can look at the photograph on *page 62* to make our pattern or make one of your own. When we made our shirt, we started with one shape and one color and stamped it on the body and sleeves of the shirt. Then we changed utensils and paint colors and did the same thing, sometimes slightly overlapping the designs.

5 Let the shirt lie flat while drying. After the shirt is dry, remove the waxed paper and enjoy wearing your one-of-a-kind shirt (or give it to a special friend).

Did you know?

✳ "T-shirts" got their name because they look like the letter "T."

Make a bracelet for yourself and one for a friend—they are easy to make and fun to wear! All you need is a zipper and some imagination! Look on the next page and learn how to make these oh-so-fun bracelets.

wear it

friendship
bracelets

64

you'll need...

Tacky glue
Star jewels
6- or 7-inch zipper
Paint pens
Velcro pieces with self-stick
    backing

1 On the fabric part of the zipper, glue star jewels in a row or make a pattern. Let the glue dry.

tip:
You can sew beads or buttons onto the zipper for decoration instead of gluing on jewels.

2 Use paint pens to make fun designs on the zipper around the jewels. Or, use the paint pens to write your favorite friends' names.

3 Wrap the zipper around your wrist, seeing where the zipper ends overlap. Cut the Velcro pieces into small squares. Peel off the backing of the self-stick Velcro and stick it to the ends of the zipper where they overlapped—two pieces on the right side and two pieces on the wrong side.

tip:
Instead of using Velcro pieces to close your bracelet, you could sew on snaps.

Did you Know?
✳ Early zippers were so expensive to make that they doubled the price of a pair of pants or a skirt.
✳ It took 20 years to perfect the design of the zipper.

mask.
mania

A little felt, paint, and glue are all you need to disguise yourself at a masquerade party. Turn the page and learn how to make our Flower Fantasy and Spaceman masks.

Did you Know?

❋ Masks are used all over the world in almost every culture to describe feelings or events.

❋ The oldest mask looked like a wild animal.

67

flower fantasy mask

you'll need...

Tracing paper
Pencil
Scissors
Fabric marking pen
Crafts glue
Felt in pink, lavender, fuchsia,
   and green
Fabric paint pens in dark pink,
   medium pink, yellow,
   and green
Plain mask

Trace your mask patterns from page 70.

1 With a pencil, trace the Flower Fantasy Mask patterns from *page 70* onto tracing paper. Use a fabric marking pen to trace around these pieces onto the felt. Cut the pieces from felt the same color as the pattern piece or choose your own colors. Cut the number of felt pieces shown on each of the pattern pieces.

2 Use the medium pink paint pen to outline the petals on the large pink flower. Also use medium pink to fill in the center and make the dots on the fuchsia flowers. Use the dark pink paint pen to fill in the centers and make the lines on the lavender flowers. Draw the veins on the leaves with green paint pen. Let the paint dry.

3 Using the photographs on *pages 66–67* as a guide, glue several leaves to the mask to cover the nose. Glue the remainder of the leaves and the flowers around the outer edge of the mask. Make sure the leaves and flowers stick out over the edge of the mask.

4 Glue the large pink flowers over the eyes, matching the eye holes. Outline the eye holes using the yellow paint pen. Let the paint dry.

tip: When you are done using your paint pen, put a straight pin in the open end before putting the cap back on. This will keep the point clog-free.

spaceman mask

Tracing paper
Pencil
Scissors
Fabric marking pen
Crafts glue
Felt in gray, royal blue, medium
    blue, and light blue
Fabric paint pens in silver
    and red
Plain mask

Trace your mask patterns from page 70.

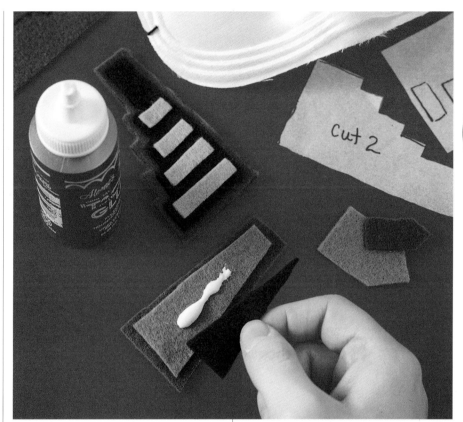

wear it

Cut 2

1 With a pencil, trace the Spaceman Mask patterns from *page 70* onto tracing paper. Use a fabric marking pen to trace around these pieces onto the felt. Cut the pieces from felt the same color as the pattern piece or choose your own favorite colors. Cut the number of felt pieces shown on each of the pattern pieces for the Spaceman Mask.

2 Glue the gray strip (piece A) to the mask, matching the eye holes. Layer the felt pieces and glue them together. Glue the layered pieces on the mask, leaving small spaces between the main pieces, so parts of the mask show through as shown in the photograph on *page 67*.

3 Add dots and lines with paint pens, using the pattern as a guide.

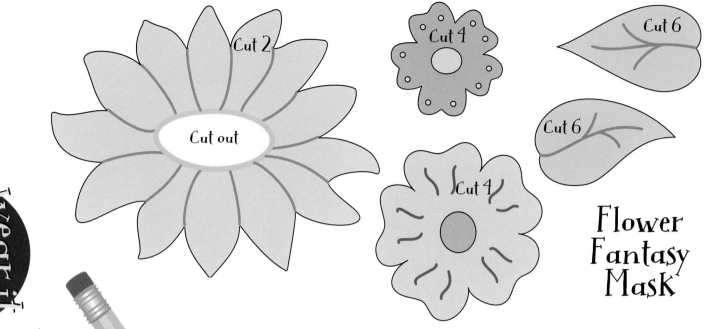

Cut 2

Cut out

Cut 4

Cut 6

Cut 6

Cut 4

Flower
Fantasy
Mask

wear it

Trace these patterns to make your masks.

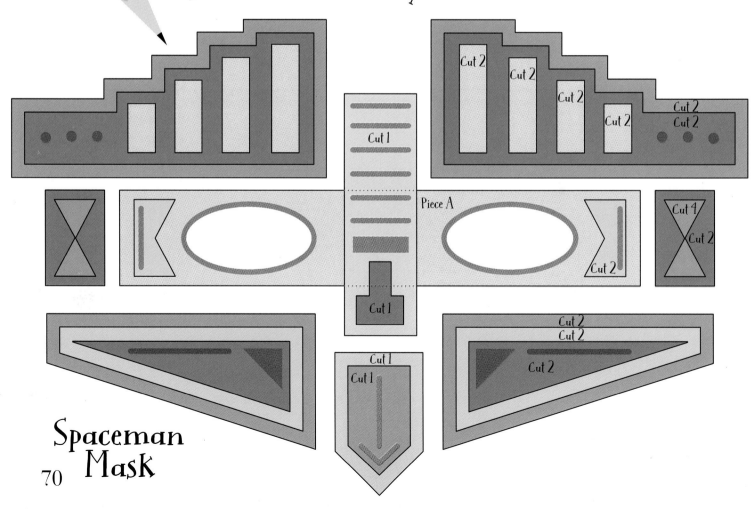

Cut 2

Cut 2

Cut 2

Cut 2

Cut 2
Cut 2

Cut 1

Cut 4

Cut 2

Cut 1

Piece A

Cut 1

Cut 2
Cut 2

Cut 2

Cut 1
Cut 1

Spaceman
Mask

puppets &dolls

to craft and love...

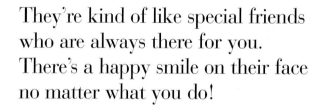

They're kind of like special friends
who are always there for you.
There's a happy smile on their face
no matter what you do!

You can make your own new friend
from cloth, or felt, or wood.
And you can name them silly names.
In fact, they think you should!

So go ahead and make a friend
and love it every day.
Because it's yours and yours alone,
it's here—and here to stay.

These puppet friends are as silly as can be. They exchange heads on the same glove body—a real split personality! To learn how to make Willy and Nilly, turn the page.

Willy & Nilly

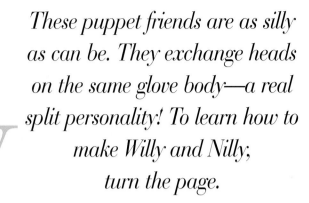

Did you Know?

✸ The person moving a puppet is called a "puppeteer."

✸ A "marionette" is a puppet on strings.

72

Willy and Nilly

you'll need...

For Willy:

Knit glove
Thread to match glove
Sewing needle
Pencil
Tracing paper
Scissors
4x6-inch piece of peach felt
2x2½-inch piece of violet felt
1x2-inch piece of red felt
1x2-inch piece of black felt
Peach sewing thread
Sewing needle
Fiberfill stuffing
Fabric glue
½x5½-inch strip of
   yellow long-pile fake fur
Two ⅝-inch-diameter plastic
   wiggle eyes
1-inch-diameter pink pom-pom
Two 1x1-inch pieces of
   Velcro
24 inches of 1½-inch-wide
   ribbon

tip:
You could use a pair of gloves and sew each head to a separate glove.

For Nilly you'll also need:

4x6-inch piece of peach felt
1x2-inch piece of violet felt
1x2-inch piece of red felt
Two ⅝-inch-diameter
   plastic wiggle eyes
Sixteen ½-inch-diameter
   brown pom-poms
2 small feathers
Two 1x1-inch pieces of Velcro
An almond in the shell

1 Tuck the fourth finger on the glove to the inside. Use matching thread to stitch the finger opening closed.

2 Turn the glove wrong side out and cut off the finger, ¼ inch from the stitching. Set the glove aside.

3 Trace one of each pattern piece from *page 75* onto tracing paper and cut out. Cut four head ovals from the peach-colored piece of felt. Cut the other felt pieces from the colors shown on the patterns.

4 Using peach thread, sew the head pieces together using a running stitch (see *below*). Sew around the edge, leaving an opening at the top.

Running Stitch

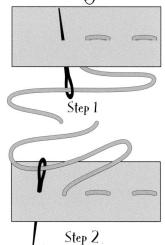

Step 1

Step 2

puppets

5 Stuff the head with fiberfill. Sew the opening closed.

6 Using the patterns *right,* and photos on *pages 72–73* as guides, glue on the face pieces and the fur or pom-pom hair.

7 Glue the hook half of one Velcro square to the tops of the two middle glove fingers. Glue the loop half on the middle of the head back. Stick a head to the fingers. For Willy, tie a bow around the middle glove fingers. Add a purse or beads to Nilly.

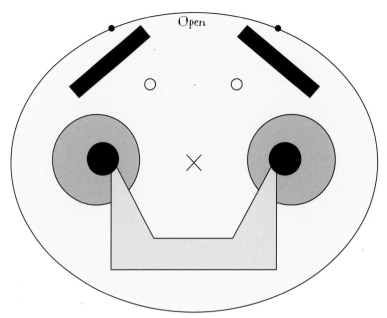

Open

Willy's Face

Trace these patterns to make your puppet's face!

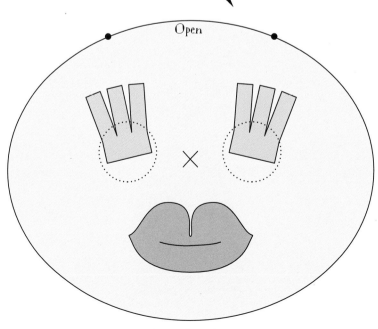

Open

Nilly's Face

75

Of course you like your vegetables—but you'll love your new vegetable doll! Complete with a body made from two packets of seeds, this handsome fellow is sure to be a favorite. The next page tells you how to make Mr. Beethead.

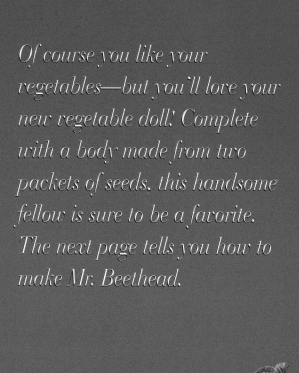

Mr. Beethead

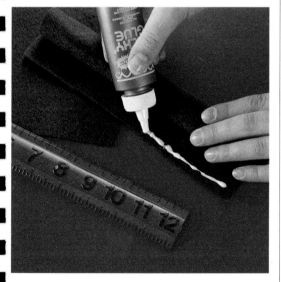

1 Cut each green felt rectangle to measure 8½x8½ inches. To make the legs, roll each piece and glue the overlapping edge in place.

2 Using 1 yard of red yarn for each leg, tie one end around the bottom of the roll 1 inch from the end, leaving a 3-inch-long tail of yarn. Wrap the yarn diagonally halfway up the leg. Reverse the wrapping to go back down the leg, creating an "X" pattern (see photograph, *above*). Tie the yarn to the tail left over at the beginning. Cut off the extra yarn.

tip:

When you glue the pieces of felt together, you'll have to hold them for a few minutes so they stick together.

3 Lay the legs side by side and glue the top 4 inches of the legs together. Leave the bottom wrapped sections free.

4 Cut the yellow felt to measure 4x11½ inches. Roll the piece lengthwise and glue the overlapping edge. Beginning ¾ inch from each end, wrap the arm roll with green yarn in the same way the legs were wrapped in Step 2.

77

Mr. Beethead

dolls

5 Glue the center of the arm roll across the top of the two legs. Bend the ends of the arm roll down and glue to the side of each leg so the arms will stay down.

6 Apply a line of glue across the top back of each seed packet. Glue one to the front and one to the back of the doll's body, placing the top edges across the arm section.

7 Glue the eyes to the vegetable or fruit. Use the black paint pen to make a mouth and eyebrows. Allow the paint to dry.

tip: If you don't have plastic wiggle eyes, you could paint on the eyes instead.

8 Glue the head to the top of the body.

Did you Know?

✳ Cornhusk dolls were made as early as 1770 and are still being made today.

bloomin' egg family

Now here's a funny and fragile family. With hair made of tiny plants, this trio is sure to bring smiles to your family! Turn the page to learn how to make our egghead bunch.

Did you Know?

* Of living birds, the ostrich lays the largest egg. It is 7 inches long and 5 inches wide, and can hold 3 quarts of liquid.
* The smallest eggs are the size of a pea and come from hummingbirds.

bloomin' egg family

dolls

you'll need...

3 eggs
Paring knife or sharp
   pointed object
1 ¼-inch-diameter
   wrapping paper tube
Ruler
Construction paper in yellow,
   turquoise, blue, black,
   white, and orange
Scissors, including
   decorative-edged scissors
   if available
Crafts glue
Tracing paper
Pencil
3 ½-inch-long strand of
   pearl beads
Two ½-inch-diameter buttons
Black ultra-fine-point
   permanent marker
Red marker
Tiny plants

1 Wash the eggs in warm soapy water, rinse, and let dry. Poke a hole in the narrow end of each egg using the knife or a pointed object.
You should ask a grown-up for a helping hand with this.

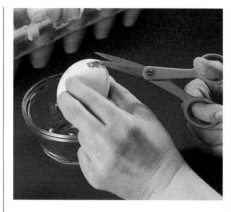

2 Enlarge the hole until a finger will fit through.

3 Using your fingers, carefully pinch off small pieces of shell around the hole, enlarging it until it is a little bigger than a quarter. Pour out the egg, rinse the shells, and set them aside to dry.

4 Cut the paper tube into a 2-inch-long tube for the father and 1⅝-inch-long tubes for the mother and the child.

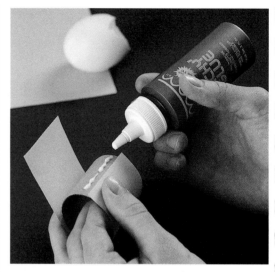

5 Cut a 2x4¼-inch black paper rectangle for the father, a 1⅝x4¼-inch turquoise paper rectangle for the mother, and a 1⅝x4¼-inch yellow paper rectangle for the child. Wrap the paper around the tube and glue the overlapping edge in place.

tip: Be sure to wash your hands often when working with eggs.

6 Trace the father's bow tie and collar from the patterns *below* onto tracing paper and cut them out. Trace around and cut the collar from white paper and the bow tie from orange paper. Glue the collar around the black tube just below the top edge. Glue the bow tie to the front of the collar.

7 Cut a ¹⁄₂x4¹⁄₄-inch strip of yellow paper. Trim one long edge with the decorative-edged scissors to make a scallop-edged collar. Glue the collar around the top edge of the turquoise tube. Glue the beads to the turquoise tube at the top edge to look like a necklace.

8 Cut three ¹⁄₈x4¹⁄₄-inch strips of blue paper. Glue them around the yellow tube to make stripes. Glue the buttons down the front.

9 Looking at the face patterns *below,* use a pencil to draw each of the faces on an egg (the open end will be at the top).

10 Go over the pencil lines using the black marker. Make the lips and rosy cheeks using the red marker.

11 Glue each of the eggs to its decorated tube. Fill the decorated eggs with dirt and plant with tiny plants.

These patterns are for your egg family.

Father

Mother

Father's Bow Tie

Child

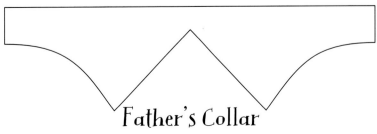

Father's Collar

There is no end to the friends you can make—all from little clothespins! You pick the color of their hair, clothes, and even the hats and shoes they wear. Learn how to make these clothespin kids and their snowman friend on the following pages.

dolls

Did you Know?

* Dolls in the 1700s were made of wood or wax.
* "Penny dolls" are jointed wooden dolls that could be bought for a penny in the 1800s.

clothespin kids & snowman

clothespin kids

dolls

you'll need...

2 small flat clothespins
Ultra-fine-tip markers OR
  acrylic paints and a small
  artist's detail brush
Ruler
2 wood craft picks
Cotton embroidery floss in
  colors chosen for dolls'
  clothing
Crafts glue
Tape
Two 3/8x1-inch wood craft
  ovals

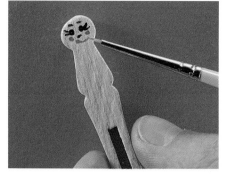

1 Draw or paint a face on each clothespin head. We used black for the eyes, lashes, eyebrows, and nose. We used red for the mouth and pink for the cheeks. You can add a tiny dot of white to each eye for a highlight. Look at *page 86* for ideas.

2 Cut a ⅞-inch-long piece off the rounded end of each craft pick for the arms.

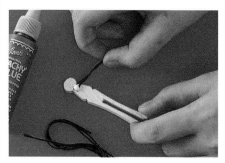

3 For each doll, choose two colors for the sweater. Start by gluing the ends of the floss to the back of the clothespin, just below the head.

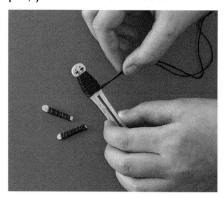

4 Hold both colors together without twisting and wrap the clothespin to the legs, making stripes. Wrap two arms to match for each doll, leaving the rounded end of the craft pick showing for the hand. Glue the arms to the shoulders.

5 Beginning at the bottom of the sweater, wrap the floss for the pants down over the hips and down each leg, ending ½ inch above the end of the clothespin.

6 Wrap the floss for the boots from the bottom of each pants leg to the end of the clothespin.

7 For the girl's hair, cut fifteen 2-inch-long strands of floss. Lay the strands side by side and tie them together in the center. Glue the center to the top of the head. Gather half of the hair on each side of the girl's head and tie with a floss bow to make pigtails.

8 For the boy's hair, cut tiny snips of floss and glue them to the top of the head.

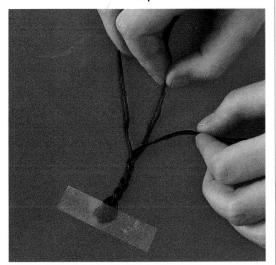

9 For each hat, cut six 8-inch-long strands of floss. Knot the strands together at one end and tape to the table. Braid the strands loosely, using two strands for each ply of the braid (see photo *above*). When the braid measures 3 inches, knot the ends. Trim the floss to ¼ inch beyond the last knot for the pom-pom. Wind and glue the braid around the top of the head starting with a circle and ending with the pom-pom on top.

10 For each doll's scarf, cut three 6-inch-long strands of floss. Knot and braid as for the hats. Tie the scarves around the dolls' necks.

11 Paint the wood ovals white and let them dry. Glue an oval to the bottom of each doll so they will stand.

12 If you like, make tiny snowballs using the clay recipe on *page 86*. Roll the clay balls in glue and then in tiny cut pieces of white floss. Glue the snowball to the dolls' hands.

Here are some other clothespin kid ideas!

dolls

85

snowman

you'll need...

1 recipe crafty clay (see *below*)
Acrylic paints in orange
  and white
Small artist's detail brush
Round toothpick
Small twig
White and black cotton
  embroidery floss
Crafts glue
Scissors
3 floss skein labels

crafty clay

you'll need...

1 cup flour
½ cup salt
½ cup hot water
Mixing bowl
Spoon

Mix the flour and salt together in the bowl. Carefully add the hot water and stir. Take the dough out of the bowl and knead it.

Have a grown-up give you a helping hand to make the clay.

1 Make the clay according to the recipe *below left*. Using the photo on *page 83* as a guide, make a snowman about 2½ inches tall, using three balls of clay. Before the clay dries, paint ½ inch of the toothpick with orange paint. Break off the painted part and poke it into the snowman's face for a nose. Break off two small pieces of the twig and poke them into the sides for arms. Let the clay snowman dry overnight.

2 Beginning at the top of the head, wrap the entire snowman with white floss, gluing as needed. Make a scarf in the same manner as for the Clothespin Kids, using six 9-inch-long strands of floss. Tie scarf around snowman's neck.

3 To make the snowman's eyes and buttons, tie a strand of black embroidery floss in five double knots, leaving spaces between each of the knots. Cut the knots apart and glue them on the snowman as shown on *page 83*.

4 Cut ½ inch off one floss skein label to make a shorter tube for the crown of the snowman's hat. Open the other two labels and lay them flat. From the flat labels, cut two circles about the size of a nickel for the brim of the hat. Glue the circles together. Glue the ½-inch-tall tube to the center of the circles to complete the hat. Glue the hat to the top of the snowman's head.

tip: You can also make your clay using the magic clay recipe on *page 60*.

mama & baby

Our mama is so proud of her baby, she carries
her little one with her everywhere she goes.
You can make this soft, cuddly couple using felt,
floss, and yarn. Turn the page and learn how.

87

dolls

mama & baby

you'll need...

Pencil
Tracing paper
Two 9x12-inch pieces of purple felt
Two 9x12-inch pieces of pink felt
9x12-inch piece of black felt
9x12-inch piece of flesh felt
Scrap of white felt
Scissors
Fabric glue
Black thread
Cotton embroidery floss in red and purple
Straight pins
Tapestry needle
Fiberfill stuffing
Two 6-inch-long strands of rug yarn for hair
4 inches of ⅛-inch-wide pink ribbon
6 assorted buttons
Cotton swab
Powder blush

tip:
There is only one sleeve piece because the mama's left arm becomes the baby.

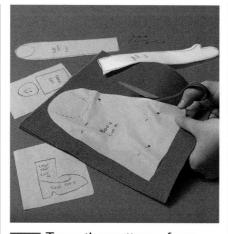

1 Trace the patterns from *pages 90-91* onto tracing paper and cut out. Cut the bodies and the sleeve from purple felt; the leg/foot pieces, right arms, and faces from pink felt; the shoes from black felt; and the left arms from flesh felt.

2 Glue the mama's face to one of the purple body pieces. Cut two pea-size circles from black felt and glue to the face for eyes. Cut two tiny snips of white felt and glue to the eyes as shown in the photograph on *page 87*. Cut a 1½-inch-long piece of black thread, dip it in glue, and shape it into a curve on the face to make the nose (see Mama's Face pattern on *page 90*). Make the mouth in the same way using 1½ inches of red floss.

3 Glue two leg/foot pieces back to back to make each leg. Glue a shoe to both sides of each leg/foot piece.

4 Glue the right arm pieces back to back. Repeat for the left arm pieces.

5 Pin the body front to back, inserting the arms and legs between the dots on the pattern. Make sure the thumb on the right arm points up.

6 Thread the needle with a strand of purple floss. Sew the body together using a running stitch (see *below*) around the edge. Leave an opening across the top of the head for stuffing.

Running Stitch

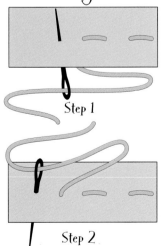

Step 1

Step 2

7 Stuff the body with fiberfill. Sew the opening closed.

8 Untwist the rug yarn pieces. Tie a knot in both ends of each piece. Glue the pieces across the top of the head for hair. Use as many pieces as you wish.

9 Glue the baby's face to the front side of the left arm. Cut two tiny black felt circles and glue to the face for eyes. Dip a ¾-inch-long piece of red floss in glue and place it on the face for a mouth. Clip a 1½-inch-long piece of yarn. Tie a bow in the center of the yarn with pink ribbon and glue it to the top of the baby's head for hair.

10 Glue the sleeve to the upper back of the right arm.

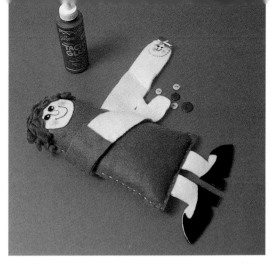

11 Cross the left arm over the right arm and fold the end of the left arm up underneath the right arm so the baby's face peeks out over the right arm. Flip the right hand up over the bottom of the baby (left arm) and glue it in place.

12 Glue the buttons to the front of the mama's dress to make polka dots.

13 Rub the cotton swab in powder blush and use it to make rosy cheeks on both of the faces (see the photo on *page 87* as a guide).

dolls

Did you Know?

☀ In the 1800s, little girls learned how to sew clothes for their dolls because dolls were often sold without clothes!

☀ Movable doll eyes weren't introduced until 1921.

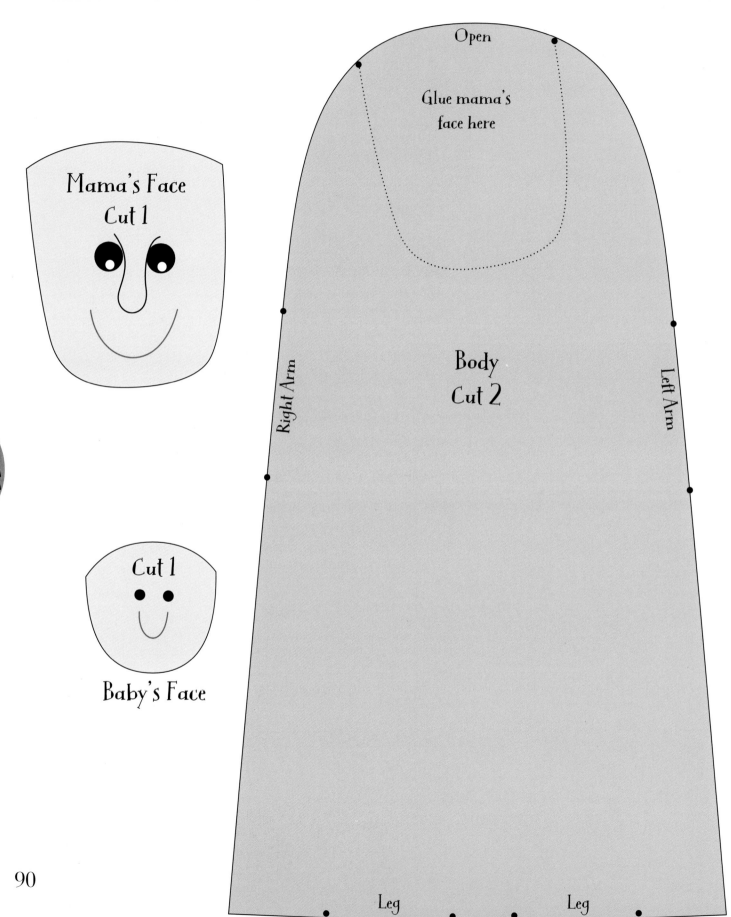

Mama's Face
Cut 1

Cut 1

Baby's Face

Open

Glue mama's
face here

Right Arm

Body
Cut 2

Left Arm

Leg

Leg

dolls

90

Right Arm
Cut 2

Sleeve
Cut 1

Glue baby's
face here

Left Arm
Cut 2

Trace these patterns to make your own mama & baby!

Leg/Foot
Cut 4

Cut here for leg/foot

Cut here for shoe

Shoe
Cut 4

Cut here for leg/foot

91

creepy
crawlers

Simply creepy, these finger puppets are a cinch to make! All you need are some pipe cleaners, wriggly eyes, and your very own fingers. Learn how to make these fuzzy friends on the next page.

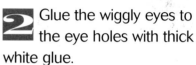

Pipe cleaners in assorted
  colors
Wiggly eyes
Thick white crafts glue

place. To make the eyes, loop
the pipe cleaner around your
finger again about 1 inch from
the first loop and twist in place;
repeat for the other eye.

2 Glue the wiggly eyes to
the eye holes with thick
white glue.

3 Bend and twist the pipe
cleaners to make each
creepy crawler different. Try
these ideas: To make corkscrew
hair, wrap a pipe cleaner
around a pencil and pull it off
the end. To make big ears,
make long loops and glue the
ends behind each eye.

Puppets

tip: Glue on small pom-poms
or jewels to dress up
your fun bugs.

1 Choose the color of
creepy crawler you want
to make. Make the loop for
your finger first by starting in
the middle of the pipe cleaner.
Wrap the pipe cleaner around
your finger and twist it to stay in

Did you Know?

❋ Pipe cleaners were originally made to
clean the stems of tobacco pipes.

pincushion
ladies

With their full skirts swirling, our delicate ladies are all dressed up in their fanciest clothes. Because they are pincushions, these fashionable ladies are useful, too!

Pencil
Tracing paper
12-inch square of fabric
Scissors or pinking shears
Acrylic paint and fine brush
    OR fine-tip markers
Doll clothespin
Doll clothespin stand
Thick white crafts glue
Doll hair
Needle and thread in
    matching color of fabric
Fiberfill
2 craft picks
12-inch piece of ⅛-inch-wide
    ribbon

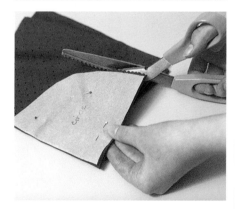

1 Trace the dress pattern from *page 97* onto tracing paper. Cut it out. Fold the fabric square in half and in half again, bringing the folds together. Place the pattern on the fabric, lining up the fold lines. Cut the curved edge with scissors or pinking shears.

2 Paint or draw a face on your doll using paint or markers (see the examples on *page 96* for ideas). Put your doll in the little doll stand.

3 Glue a strand (about 4 inches long) of doll hair to the top of the clothespin. Wrap it around the head and glue it for a bun or leave it long if you wish.

tip: Clothespin doll materials are available in the crafts departments of discount stores and in crafts stores.

4 Thread the needle with about 24 inches of thread. Knot both ends together. Use a running stitch (see *page 97*) to sew around the circle about ½ inch from the edge. Try to keep your stitches about ¼ to ½ inch in length. DO NOT cut the thread. Leave it in the needle. You will be pulling the thread to gather the skirt around the doll.

dolls

Did you Know?

✸ In 1866, some doll heads were made of leather and were sold as heads only— the doll bodies were to be made at home.

pincushion ladies

Here are some ideas for faces for your pincushion dolls!

5 Stand your clothespin doll in the center of the fabric circle and gently pull the thread. At the same time, fill the skirt with fiberfill until it is firm. Gather the skirt tightly around the waist of the doll and sew the thread back and forth to keep it from slipping. Add a little glue under the fabric.

6 Cut off about 1 inch from the rounded end of the craft picks and glue them to the sides of the doll for arms. Tie the narrow ribbon around the waist and tie a bow. Trim the ribbon ends if needed. Tie a little ribbon bow and glue it in the hair, trimming the ends of the ribbon.

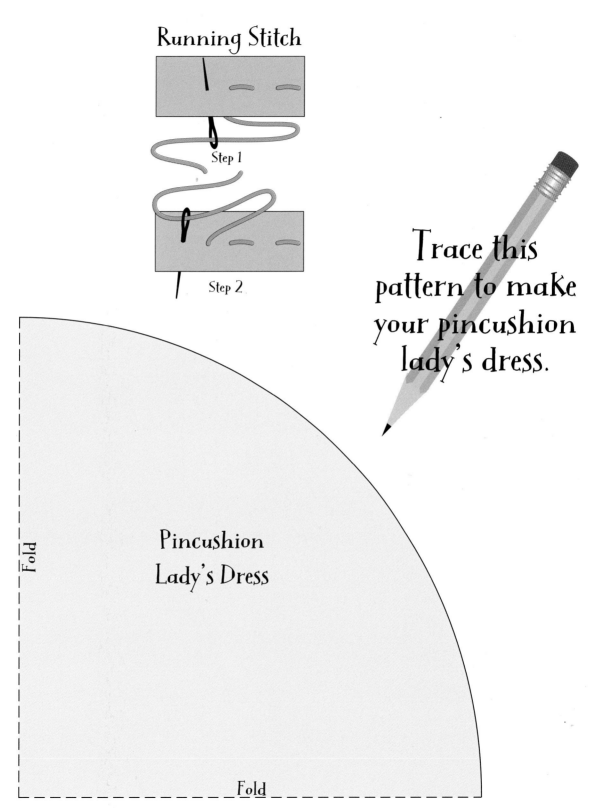

Running Stitch

Step 1

Step 2

Trace this pattern to make your pincushion lady's dress.

Fold

Pincushion Lady's Dress

Fold

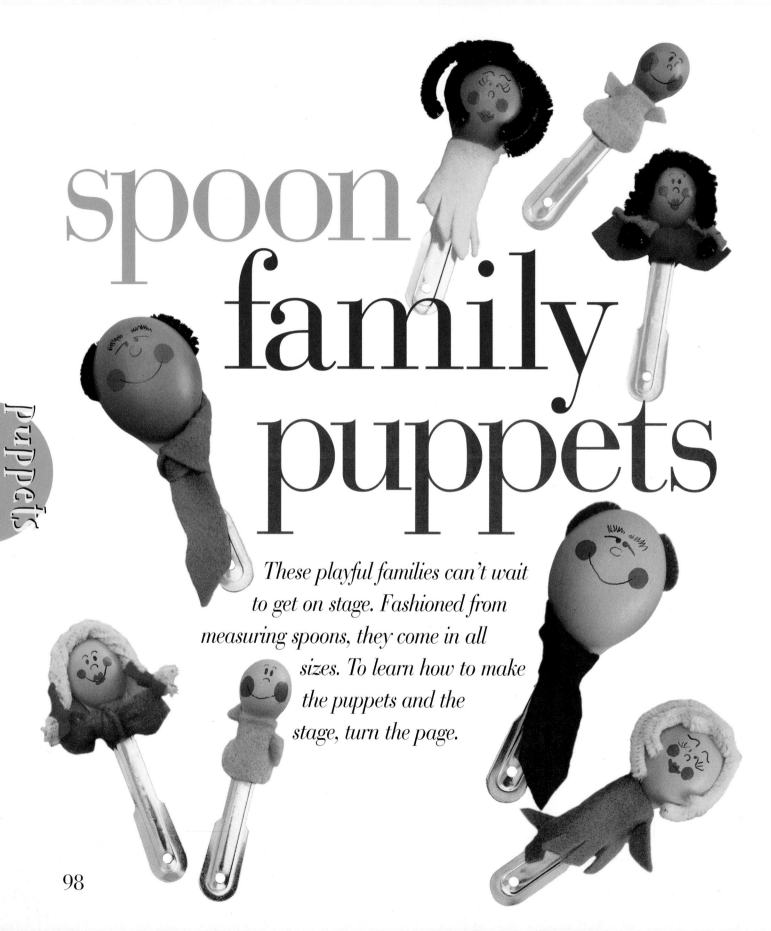

spoon family puppets

These playful families can't wait to get on stage. Fashioned from measuring spoons, they come in all sizes. To learn how to make the puppets and the stage, turn the page.

Did you Know?

☀ Early dolls had crude wooden hands called "spoon hands."

99

spoon family puppets

2 Using the patterns on *page 101* as a guide, draw faces on each spoon using the black permanent marker.

3 Trace the clothing patterns using a pencil and tracing paper. Cut out the patterns.

4 Draw around the pattern pieces on felt scraps, using whatever colors of felt you like. Cut out the felt clothing around the traced markings.

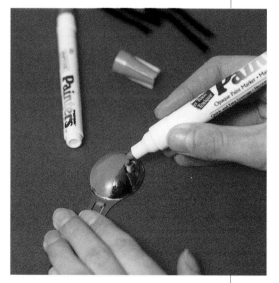

1 Color the back of the spoons using a skin-tone opaque marker. Let it dry and color on a second coat. Let dry.

5 Tie the felt bib onto the baby, using a drop of crafts glue to hold it in place. Let the glue dry.

6 Tie the scarf onto the big sister spoon and put a drop of glue under the felt to hold it in place. Let the glue dry.

7 Tie the scarf onto the mom and put a drop of glue under the felt to hold it in place. Let the glue dry.

8 Tie the necktie onto the dad and put a drop of glue under the felt to hold it in place. Let the glue dry.

9 Choose a pipe cleaner color for the big sister's hair. Cut the pipe cleaner into three equal pieces. Twist the pieces together and shape to the top of the spoon. Tie small scraps of felt at each end for bows. Glue the hair to the top of head.

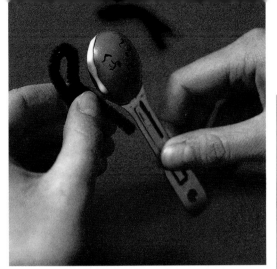

10 Choose a pipe cleaner color for the mom's hair. Cut one 3-inch length and one 4-inch length of pipe cleaner. Fold the pieces in half. On the 4-inch piece, fold the loop end over to make bangs. Glue the hair pieces to each side of the head.

11 Choose a pipe cleaner color for dad's hair. Cut two 1-inch lengths. Bend the ends and glue one piece of hair to each side of the head.

tip: You could use tiny ribbons, jewels, or markers to decorate the family's clothes.

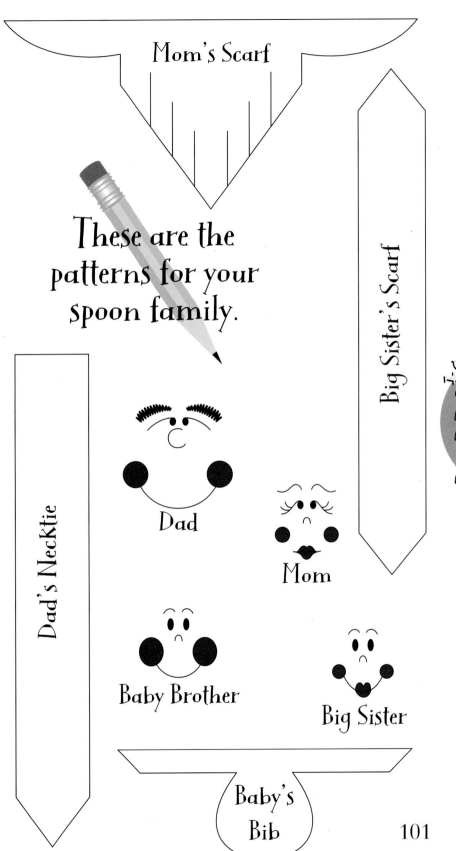

Mom's Scarf

These are the patterns for your spoon family.

Big Sister's Scarf

Dad's Necktie

Dad

Mom

Baby Brother

Big Sister

Baby's Bib

Puppets

101

puppet stage

you'll need...

Shoe box with lid
Scissors
Paper punch
Crafts glue
Acrylic paints in two colors
Paintbrush
36-inch-long piece of yarn
Photograph stickers
Paper napkins or two
   6x6-inch scraps of fabric
Paper clips

1 Cut the bottom out of the shoe box using scissors. Ask a grown-up for a helping hand with this.

2 Using the picture *below*, punch two holes at the top of the short ends of the shoe box (about an inch apart and opposite each other).

3 Cut off one long side of the shoebox lid. Lay the lid with the sides pointing up.

4 Spread glue on the outside of the long side of the shoe box that is farthest away from the punched holes. With the glue side down, press the shoe box to the lid, lining up the cut edge of lid with the uncut edge of the box (see the photo on *page 99*). Let the glue dry.

5 Use whatever color of paint you like to paint the inside and floor of the stage. Apply as many coats as needed to cover up any writing on your shoe box. (Be sure to let the box dry between coats!)

6 Paint the outside of the stage using a different color of paint. Again, paint on more than one coat if needed to cover up the markings on shoe box. Let the paint dry.

Puppet Stage

7 Thread the yarn through punched holes as shown *above*. Pull the yarn carefully so the top of the stage curves. Tie the ends into a knot.

8 To make a curtain for the stage, fold the napkin or fabric scraps like a fan and use paper clips to hang them from the yarn.

9 Decorate the outside of the stage however you like, using funny photograph caption stickers, gems, more paints—whatever you think is fun!

tip: When punching the holes, punch through the shoe box edge that has only a single layer of cardboard.

one, two, three

paint!

Red, yellow,
green, and blue,
get out the brushes—
there's so much to do!

It's your masterpiece and
you can't wait to start.
Anything YOU make
is a work of art!

Dip it, stripe it,
dot it, too!
Don't be afraid to
try something new.

Happy Mother's Day

Happy Birthday!

paint

happy cards

You could start your own card business with these no-fail cards designed by you! To learn how to make these one-of-a-kind originals, just turn the page.

Did you Know?

✸ The first greeting cards were used in Egypt in the sixth century B.C. and were added to New Year's gifts.

Happy

Happy

Happy
Mother's Day

Happy Birthd

To: Dad

From: Joe

happy cards

you'll need...

Typing paper
Paintbrush
Tempera or
    liquid acrylic paints
Purchased blank greeting
    cards
Colored markers

paint

1 Fold the piece of typing paper in half and crease the fold. Fold the paper in half again, bringing the folded edges together, and crease.

2 Open the piece of paper. Using a paintbrush and at least three colors, put a dot or glob (not too much!) of each paint in the center of the paper where the folds are. Try to use colors that blend well when mixed together. Look at the color wheel and the color mixing guide on *page 107* for help.

Did you Know?

※ The largest greeting card company makes about 14,000 new card designs each year.

106

3 Fold the paper again as you did in Step 1 and gently rub the colors together. Open up the paper.

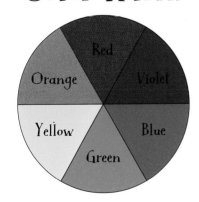

tip:
Don't take too long rubbing the paint or it will begin to dry and may stick.

4 Turn the paper upside down on the front of the card and rub the paper gently. Pull the top paper off of the card.

5 Let the card dry. Using a marker, write a greeting on the front or inside of the card.

Color Wheel

Red
Orange
Violet
Yellow
Blue
Green

Color Mixing Guide

Red + Yellow = Orange

Red + Blue = Violet

Yellow + Blue = Green

Red + White = Pink

Black + White = Gray

Blue + Black = Navy Blue

Orange + Green = Brown

"egg-ceptional" eggs

Gather some pencils, a toothbrush, adhesive bandages, and toothpicks, and you're ready to decorate eggs! Sound crazy? Look on the next page to see how these everyday things will help you make the most stunning and colorful eggs.

you'll need...

Hard-boiled eggs (prepared
by a grown-up)
Cardboard paper towel roll
Masking tape
Acrylic paint in colors you like
Disposable plate
Toothbrush
Toothpicks
Pencil with new eraser
Adhesive bandages

For all the eggs:

If you want the background
color to be the natural
white (or brown) of the
eggshell, just decorate a
plain egg. For other colors,
paint the egg a solid color
and let it dry. Painting an
egg is tricky because it
wants to roll all over the
table. You can use your
creativity to keep it from
rolling—we used a short
tube cut from a paper
towel roll and taped it to
the table to make a stand.
Or, you can paint the top
half of the egg and put it
back in the egg carton, let
it dry, turn it over, and
paint the other side.

**We used four different ways
to decorate these eggs:**

toothbrush

1 Pour some paint onto a
disposable plate. Dip
JUST THE END of the toothbrush
bristles into the paint and dot the
egg with the paint. Let one side
dry, and then do the other side.

tip:
DO NOT eat eggs that
are not refrigerated or are
decorated with paint.

toothpicks

1 Choose two colors of
paint to decorate your
egg and pour those paints on
the disposable plate. To make
the petals of the flower, dip
about ¼ inch of the toothpick
into the paint then lay the
toothpick down onto the egg,
making a petal. Repeat making
petals as shown, *above*, leaving
a space in the middle for the
flower center. Using a new
toothpick and another color of
paint, dip JUST THE TIP of the
toothpick in the paint and dot
the center two or three times.
Let the egg dry.

paint

"egg-ceptional" eggs

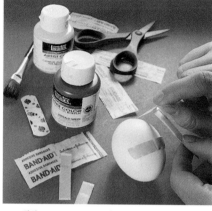

pencil

1 Pour some paint onto a disposable plate. Dip just the end of the eraser into the paint and dot the egg. Wash or wipe off the eraser to change colors. Dot one color at a time. Cover the egg with dots.

tip:
You can also use a cotton swab to make small dots on your egg.

adhesive bandages

1 This way of decorating your egg works best on a natural-colored egg instead of painting the egg first. Cut larger bandages in half the long way or use small bandages to decorate the egg. Overlap the bandage strips or make whatever design you choose.

2 Paint the entire egg, covering all of the bandages. Let the egg dry.

3 Carefully peel off the adhesive bandages. There will be eggshell-colored stripes where the bandages were.

tip:
You could make designs on the eggshell-colored stripes by using some of the other painting ideas.

paint

Did you Know?

✳ The duckbill platypus and the spiny anteater are the only mammals that lay eggs.

Did you Know?

❋ The bullfrog sheds (that is like laying) 10,000 to 25,000 eggs in one season.

Paint

111

veggie print wraps

Are there vegetables left in your refrigerator?
If you didn't eat them all for dinner—paint with them!
To learn how to make your own colorful wrapping
papers by printing with vegetables,
turn the page.

paint

veggie print wraps

Newspapers
Raw firm vegetables and fruits
    such as carrots, celery,
    peppers, artichokes,
    apples, and pears
Sharp knife
Acrylic paint in colors you like
Disposable plate
Plain-colored wrapping papers,
    paper sacks, or newsprint
    papers

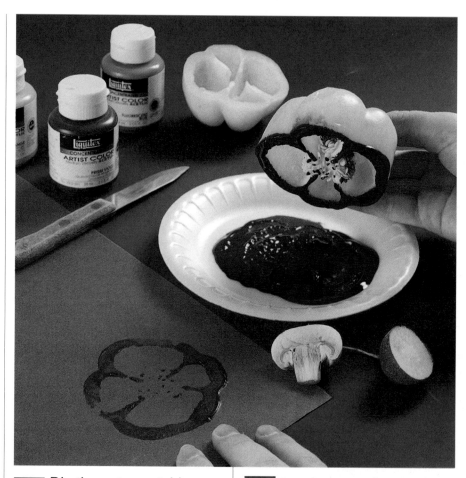

Paint

1 Cover your work surface with newspapers.

2 Have a grown-up give you a helping hand to cut the vegetables or fruits in half with a sharp knife. You will get a different design depending on the direction you cut the vegetables or fruits. It is important that the larger vegetables and fruits are cut very straight so the paint will cover them evenly when they are dipped into the paint.

3 Pour some paint onto the plate and spread it around to make a smooth, thin surface.

4 Dip the cut vegetable or fruit into the paint and practice printing on paper sacks, newsprint, or newspaper. Don't use too much paint or the design will run together. You can wash the vegetable and use it in another color of paint, if you wish.

5 Lay the wrapping paper on the table. After you like how your vegetable or fruit is printing, dip it into the paint and press it firmly on the paper. Repeat the design all over the paper until you like what you see!

6 Let the paper dry. For gift wrapping ideas using your paper, see *page 115*.

114

Did you Know?

* A dried gourd was probably the first rattle and may be the oldest-known toy.

* Any vegetables that grow under the ground, such as potatoes, are called "tubers."

tip:
You can also use stamped papers for place mats, greeting cards, and pieces of artwork to be framed!

Paint

115

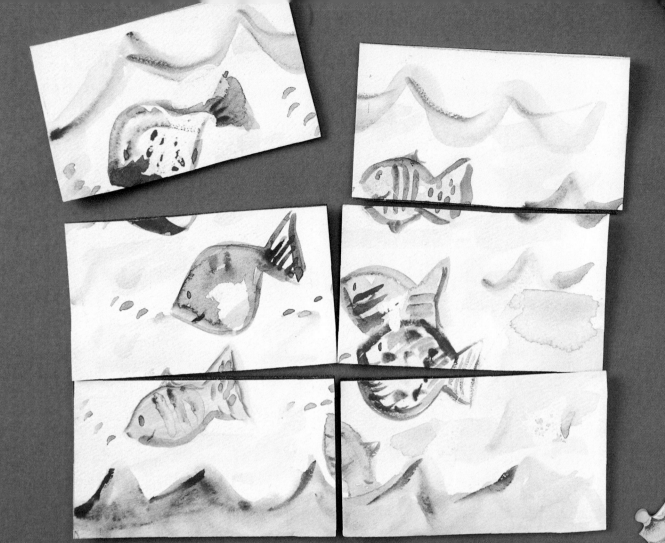

paint

stick-to-it puzzle

Here is a puzzle that will stick with you. Paint an original work of
art using some of our watercolor tips, and then turn your masterpiece
into a magnetic puzzle. To learn how, see the next page.

116

you'll need...

Watercolor paper
Scissors
Masking tape
Watercolor paints
Water in dish
Paintbrush
Pencil
Ruler
Rubber cement or crayons
Paper towels
3½x2-inch self-stick magnets
    made for attaching
    business cards (available
    at office supply stores and
    discount stores)

1 Decide how big you want to make your puzzle. (After your puzzle is done, each piece will be as big as one magnet.) Cut a piece of paper ½ inch larger on all sides than the finished puzzle. (We used six of the self-stick magnets for our puzzle. The piece of paper we cut was 8x7 inches. We trimmed ½ inch from all of the sides where we had put tape and that made our finished puzzle 7x6 inches.)

2 Tape the watercolor paper to the table or to a board. Paint your picture any way you wish. Try using some of the watercolor techniques we've shown on *pages 118–119.*

3 Let your picture dry and remove the tape.

painting with watercolor

Painting with watercolor paints is fun. Have you ever noticed that the paper seems to wrinkle after the paint is dry? To keep this from happening, use masking tape to tape your piece of paper all around the edges to a board or table. Leave the painting there and let it dry before you remove the tape.

4 Using a pencil and ruler, mark your picture where it is to be cut. Each piece should fit on one magnet. Cut out the pieces with your scissors.

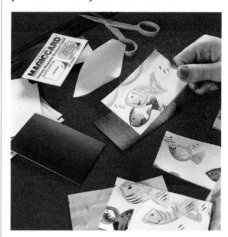

5 Peel off the backing on the magnets and attach the magnets to the back of each piece of the puzzle.

6 Try putting the pieces of the puzzle together and then put them on the refrigerator for everyone to try!

117

watercolor techniques

You may paint your picture any way you wish, but here are some fun watercolor techniques to try:

rubber cement resist painting

1 Before you start painting, drizzle some rubber cement on the paper wherever you want the paper to stay white after you paint.

2 Let the rubber cement dry. Now paint over the rubber cement as if it weren't there. Let the watercolor paint dry completely.

3 Using your finger, rub the rubber cement off of the painting. It will leave nice white highlights on your picture.

Did you Know?

☀ The first artist to experiment and paint with watercolors was German master Albrecht Dürer in the 1500s.

☀ The earliest watercolor painting, called a "fresco," was paint applied to damp, fresh plaster.

paint

118

crayon resist painting

1 Before you start painting, draw some of your picture with crayon.

2 Paint directly over the crayon. The crayon will show through the paint and make an interesting picture.

wet on wet

1 Paint part of your picture using clear water. Using your paintbrush, drop in the colors you wish. Your paint will run into the water on the paper and make a soft look.

tip: Try sprinkling salt over a watercolor painting—it will look like tiny snowflakes.

dry brush

1 This technique is used when you want to put details in your picture. Paint your picture as you wish. After the picture is nearly dry, add the details. Your brush should be damp but not wet. Dry it off with a paper towel if you need to. Using thicker watercolor paint, brush on the details by moving your brush quickly.

paint

119

paint

Brainbow bookworm

*It's always fun to have a friend to read with—
and our painted and spectacled bookworm is waiting for you!
Make him with plastic foam balls and lots of colorful paint.*

1 Using a table knife, cut four of the plastic foam balls in half and place on your work surface with the flat sides down.

2 Push one end of a toothpick into the center of one plastic foam ball. Stick the other end into one of the cut balls. This will make it easier to paint your ball and keep it from rolling afterwards. Do the same with all of the other whole balls, painting each ball a different color. Let the paint dry (this may take an hour or so) and remove the toothpicks.

3 To make the bookworm's antennae, fold one yellow pipe cleaner in half and form the ends into spirals.

4 Insert the antennae where they were folded in the top of the ball you are using for the head. Glue the eyes and the pom-pom nose to the face, looking at the photograph on *page 120* to guide you.

Paint

tip: Be sure to wash your paintbrush using soap and water before changing colors.

rainbow bookworm

5 Cut the rest of the pipe cleaners in half. Fold each piece in half, twisting the ends together. Fold these pieces into "Z" shapes to make the feet. Matching pipe cleaner colors to those on the painted plastic foam balls, insert the ends of the pipe cleaner feet into the balls, using the photo on *page 120* as a guide.

6 To connect the balls, put a dot of glue on one end of a toothpick and push it into one of the painted balls. Push the other end into a second ball. Put all seven balls together in the same way, using the photo *above*, as a guide. Let the glue dry.

Did you Know?

✳ Giant earthworms can grow as long as 10 feet.

✳ Early paints were sometimes made from mixing color with egg whites or beeswax.

7 Using craft wire, form a circle the size of a nickel about 2 inches from one end. Repeat making a second circle next to the first. Bend the ends to make bows for the glasses. Center the glasses over the bookworm's eyes and push the wire ends into the head.

paint

gifts
to make all by yourself!

Keep it a secret,
don't tell a soul.
You're making a present,
it's under control!

You have what you need,
you've thought it all through.
Now make it—enjoy it!
You know what to do!

Giving a gift
is still the best part.
'Cause a present that you make
is one from your heart!

posy pins

Mom will want to wear this pretty corsage everywhere!
Choose colors that will match her coat or dress, and
give her the pin for a special occasion. To learn how
to make these springlike bouquets, see the next page.

Bunches of tiny fabric flowers
Fabric leaves on wire stems
Utility scissors
Green florist's tape
2-inch piece of ¼-inch-wide
    balsa wood
1½-inch-long pin back
Crafts glue

1 Choose a tiny bunch of flowers from the purchased bunches to make your pin. If you wish, arrange two or three leaves with your flower bunch. Trim the flower and leaf stems to measure about 2 inches long. Wrap the stems with the florist's tape. After wrapping to

the bottom of the stems, wrap back up to the top and trim the tape.

2 Wrap the tiny piece of balsa wood with the florist's tape.

3 Using the florist's tape, wrap the wrapped balsa-wood piece to the wrapped bunch of flowers.

4 Glue the back of the pin to the back side of the wrapped stems and balsa wood. Let the glue dry.

tip: If you would like to add a bow to your tiny bouquet, slip a piece of ribbon through the pin back and tie a bow in the front.

Did you Know?

* Long ago, aquamarine gems were used in jewelry to wish the wearer a happy marriage.
* Jewelry is called "costume jewelry" when there are many pieces of the same style made and they are not very expensive.

gifts

Did you Know?

✳ The sun is a glowing ball of gases about 865,000 miles in diameter.

✳ The first dark glasses, made of smoky quartz, were created by the Chinese in the early 12th century.

made
for shades

It is always fun to show off a pretty glasses case, and these are sure to be show-offs. Made with bright foam pieces, beads, and laces, they will keep those shades from breaking. Learn how to make them on the next page.

you'll need...

For purple case:

- Purple fun foam
- Scissors
- Ruler
- Ink pen or permanent marker
- Small paper punch
- 30-inch piece of red round flexible craft lacing
- 16 plastic 13-mm star beads in desired colors

For turquoise case you'll also need:

- Turquoise fun foam
- 30-inch piece of yellow round flexible craft lacing
- 32 plastic pony beads in colors that you like

1 For either project, use a ruler and pen to measure and mark two 6¾x4-inch pieces on the foam. Cut them out.

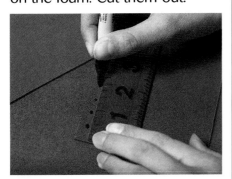

2 Starting with one long side of one piece of foam,

make a pen mark every ½ inch, approximately ¼ inch from the edge. Repeat on the opposite side and at the bottom. Leave the top of the foam unmarked.

3 Use a paper punch to punch holes where you made ink marks.

4 To mark the second foam piece, lay the punched piece over it with the edges even. Put a pen mark through each hole. Use a paper punch again to punch the holes.

5 Place one piece of foam on top of the other, matching up the holes. Push the lacing through one set of

top holes just below the unpunched edge. Tie the ends in a knot on the back side. Push the long end of the lacing back through the first hole to the front.

6 FOR THE PURPLE CASE: Thread a star bead on the lacing and push the lacing through the second hole. Bring the lacing to the front through the next hole and add another star. Do this until all the holes are laced.
FOR THE TURQUOISE CASE: Thread a pony bead on the lacing. Bring the lacing around the edge to the back and come up through the second hole and add another pony bead. Do this until all the holes are laced.

7 When the last bead is on, knot the lace on the back side and clip the end about ¼ inch from the knot.

gifts

sticks and stones

Sticks and stones won't break any bones—they'll combine to make a very clever picture frame. Paint a landscape, frame it, and give it to Dad! To learn how to make this natural-looking frame, see the next page.

you'll need...

Sticks, stones, leaves and
  other small natural things
Cardboard or purchased mat
Scissors
Glue stick
Paper punch or sharp utensil
Twine
Thick crafts glue

1 Gather your favorite small sticks, a few stones, and leaves. The leaves work best if they are small and flat.

2 Cut a frame out of cardboard with the center cut out a little smaller than the size of the picture you want to frame. Make the frame about 2 inches wide all the way around.
✋ Get a grown-up to give you a helping hand cutting out the middle of the cardboard. (Or, you can use a purchased cardboard mat. You can buy these at drugstores, discount stores, or dime stores for about a dollar.)

tip:
Go for a nature walk and find other things to glue on your frame such as acorns or seed pods.

3 Use the glue stick to glue overlapping leaves all over the front of the frame.

4 Punch or poke a hole in each corner of the frame.
✋ Get a grown-up to give you a helping hand with this. Thread a piece of twine, about 10 inches long, through each hole and tie a double knot leaving the tails of the twine long.

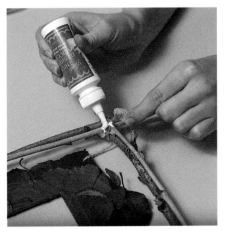

5 Choose sticks that are a little bigger than the frame. Group two together on each side, making a rectangle with overlapping corners. Wrap a 12-inch piece of twine around the sticks where they meet at the corners. Knot the ends.

6 Use the twine tails to tie the frames together at corners.

7 Glue the rocks over the twine in the corners.

Did you Know?
❋ One of the fastest growing trees is the poplar tree.
❋ The rocks in your backyard may have been formed 4.6 billion years ago.

fancy flowerpots

They hold flowers or gadgets, toothpicks or crayons—most anything around the house! These fun-to-make clay pots are the perfect gift for just about anyone and are great for showing off favorite things. To learn how to make them, turn the page.

Did you Know?

❋ Common flowerpots are made out of "terra-cotta," which means "baked earth" in Italian.

❋ Flowerpots have holes in the bottoms so water can drain out.

fancy flowerpots

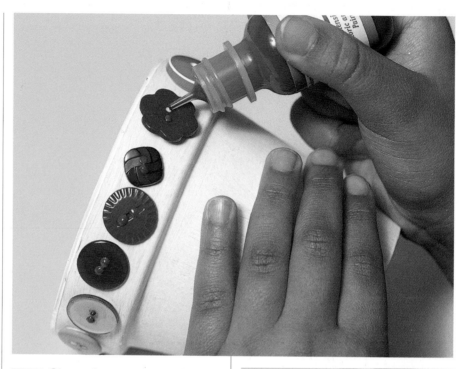

1 Use the flat brush to paint the outside of the clay pot with white paint. Let the paint dry.

2 Glue whatever colorful buttons you like around the top of the painted clay pot, leaving a small space between each of the buttons. Let the glue dry. Using paint pens in the color or colors you choose, put dots of paint over the holes in the buttons.

3 Use the round brush to paint green stems and leaves below each button.

tip:
You can lay a button on each side of the flowerpot to keep it from rolling when you're painting.

gifts

shivering shakers

Now you can make your own glitter shakers using an old jar and corn syrup. We've made our ghoulish gifts spooky and silly, but you can make them any way you wish. To learn how, turn the page.

To: Eddie

gifts

shivering shakers

1 If you want to have a figure in your shaker, glue it to the inside of the lid with thick tacky glue. Let it dry overnight.

2 Fill the jar almost to the top with corn syrup. If the syrup seems too heavy for the glitter or confetti, add a drop or two of water.

tip: Try the lid on before gluing it to see if you like how the small pieces float in the shaker. You can always change or add more things.

gifts

3 Sprinkle the confetti, glitter, wiggle eyes, or whatever you want to float in the shaker into the syrup.

tip:
Leave out the figure and add charms, pennies, marbles, or any other tiny items that won't dissolve in the shakers.

4 Put glue all around the top of the jar. Screw the lid with the glued-on figure onto the jar. Let the glue dry.

Did you Know?

✳ Corn is actually an ingredient in making clear corn syrup as well as an ingredient in making car fuel!

✳ Glitter sparkles because it reflects light.

gifts

rock
stars

With just a little crayon, these plain old rocks become stars in no time. Give them as paperweights or just to display. Learn how to make them on the next page.

you'll need...

Rocks
Crayons
Metal pan covered with foil
Old sock

1 Choose a rock with a fairly smooth surface. Color it any way you wish. Use as much crayon on the rock as you can. The more crayon you put on the rock, the prettier it will be.

tip: Experiment with different types of rocks. Some rocks like to be colored more than others!

2 Place the rocks on a foil-covered pan and put them in the oven for 15 minutes at 200°. Let the rocks cool after they come out of the oven.

🖐 Get a helping hand from a grown-up when putting the rocks in and taking them out of the oven.

3 Using an old sock, polish the rocks. This will make the melted crayon shine a little more.

Did you Know?

✳ The first rock art, which was carving on cave walls, can be traced all the way back to 30,000 B.C.

✳ "The Stone Age" was thousands of years ago when all tools and weapons were made of stone, bone, antler, ivory, or wood.

gifts

137

cool key chains

Here's a gift that is sure to win the key to any heart!
Purchased clay that you bake in the oven makes colorful
and clever key chains. Learn how to make
them on the next page.

you'll need...

Typing paper

Pencil

Key chain ring with plastic name tag

Scissors

Oven-hardening modeling clay such as Fimo or Sculpey

Wax paper

Cardboard

Rolling pin

Table knife

Cookie sheet covered with aluminum foil

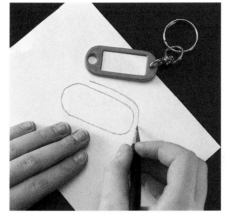

1 Draw around the key chain name tag onto typing paper. Draw another line ⅛ inch outside the first outline.

2 Cut along the second outline to make the pattern.

3 Cover the work surface with wax paper. Knead the clay until it is soft and pliable, making sure you will have enough to cover the name tag. Choose one color, or choose a combination of colors for a marbled or striped name tag.

tip: Always wash your hands before working with clay, and each time you work with a new color. Make sure your hands are dry.

tip: Make marbled and swirled clay by twisting and kneading two or more colors together until you like the effect.

4 Use the rolling pin to roll the clay into a rectangle large enough to cover both sides of the name tag. The rolled clay should be about ⅛ inch thick.

tip: Extra clay stays fresh when stored in a tightly sealed plastic bag.

Did you Know?

✳ The clay used to make pottery is found near river beds.

gifts

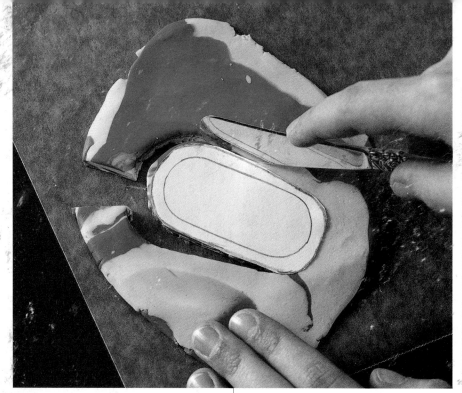

5 Using the paper pattern and the table knife, cut a clay piece to cover each side of the name tag. Cut a notch like a "V" in one end of each piece so the key ring will be able to move freely after the tag is covered.

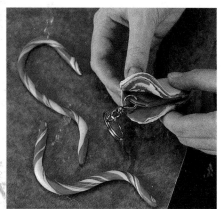

6 Sandwich the tag between the pieces of clay with the notches around the ring. Pinch the edges together and smooth the seams with your fingers.

7 You may decorate the covered name tag any way you wish. We've made a rope of swirled colors around the outer edge and a clay rope cut to make letters.

8 When the design is complete, lay the key chain on the foil-covered cookie sheet. Bake at 225° for 20 minutes. Let the key chain cool.

Ask a grown-up for a helping hand when putting the key chains in and taking them out of the oven.

tip: Make swirled clay ropes by rolling each color into a long rope. Lay the ropes side by side and twist them together. You can also slice these ropes!

Did you Know?

✳ A "locksmith" repairs locks and makes keys.

a note to parents...

Welcome to the all-new, "kid-tested" (and loved!) crafts book for kids! Designed for children 7 to 14 years of age, this exciting book will inspire children to become even more creative and independent, and to learn new skills that will help them throughout their developing years.

Most of these no-fail projects can be completed by a child with little or no supervision. However, there are a few projects you will need to assist your child with (we've marked these steps with red "Helping Hands" 👋). You'll find crafting together is a very special way to spend your time.

To spark your child's imagination, talk about picking their favorite colors, using the full-size patterns for other projects (there are more than 40 in this book), and putting their own personality into every project. It won't be long before your child will be crafting one-of-a-kind, full-of-pride projects!

We're glad you chose the *More Incredibly Awesome Crafts for Kids* book for your child. We guarantee it will get used over and over again—most likely by the whole family!

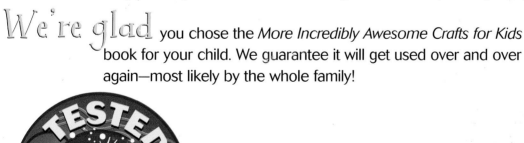

index of incredibly awesome crafts...

index

index

acknowledgments

We'd like to thank all of the fun-loving folks who enjoyed adding their creative flair to this awesome book for kids.

Designers

Nancy Bell Anderson:
  Sparkly Snowflakes 8
  Clothespin Kids &
    Snowman 82
  Pincushion Ladies 94
  Spoon Family Puppets 98

Susan Banker:
  Magic Garlands 19
  Flower Garden Vest 42
  Stamp-It Fun Shirt 62
  Spoon Family Puppets 98
  Puppet Stage 102
  Rainbow Bookworm 120
  Made for Shades 126

Kyle Benna:
  Bertram the Bird Piñata 25
  Sticks and Stones 128

Carol Field Dahlstrom:
  Magic Garlands 19
  Bedazzling Beads 58
  Friendship Bracelets 64
  Happy Cards 104
  "Egg-ceptional" Eggs 108
  Veggie Print Wraps 112
  Stick-to-It Puzzle 116
  Shivering Shakers 133
  Rock Stars 136

Phyllis Dunstan:
  Button Bracelets 38
  Picture Pals 30
  Cartoon Sneakers 50
  Willy & Nilly 72
  Mr. Beethead 76
  Bloomin' Egg Family 79
  Mama & Baby 87
  Fancy Flowerpots 130

Heather Bell Henry:
  Treasure Boxes 16

Mary Anna Lanigan:
  Friendship Bracelets 64

Karen Taylor:
  Pinwheel Pizzazz 12
  Glamour Rings 44
  Lively Laces 48
  Nature Caps 54
  Flower Fantasy and
    Spaceman Masks 68
  Creepy Crawlers 92
  Posy Pins 124
  Cool Key Chains 138

Photographers

Hopkins Associates, pages 42, 50, 57–59, 62, 73, 76, 82–83, 87, 92, 99, 108, 112–113, 116, 133, 138; Scott Little, pages 8–9, 12–13, 16, 19–20, 24–25, 30–31, 38, 44, 47, 53–54, 64, 66–67, 79, 94, 105, 120, 124, 126, 131, 136; Andy Lyons, cover and page 128. Drop-outs: Hopkins Associates, Scott Little, and Andy Lyons. Photo styling assistant: Donna Chesnut.

Models

Betty Bann, Cierra Cason, Carlie Chesnut, Alissa Clapper, Sarah Clapper, Elizabeth Dahlstrom, Drew DeJong, Kim Hutchison, Sarah Hutchison, Michelle Kaiser, Ryan Kenes, Brittany Kirk, Lindsay Lang, Chris Lorenz, Jessica Lorenz, Stacy Lorenz, Tyler Miller, Jennifer Morris, Kimberly Morris, Kelli Rae Powell, Karissa Richardson, Lindsey Richardson, Jessica Stumme, Holly Tredway, Sara Voy, Nicholas Wallace, Zachary Wallace, Sharaine Weathers